JESUS 2000

A Walk with Jesus in the Holy Land

KIRSCHNER ENTERPRISES

JESUS 2000
Y. Salomon   M. Milner

Photography: M. Milner
Design: Y. Salomon
Concept and Text: D. Salomon
English Editor: D. Camiel

© Copyright by Alfa Communication Ltd., 1998
Tel. 972-3-5794141, Fax. 972-3-5798977
Photos: © Copyright by M. Milner & Y. Salomon

Distribution:

Kirschner Enterprises
Dallas TX 75230
Tel. 972-239-9932, Fax. 214-351-4322

ISBN 965-708203-X

Pre-press: Graphor Ltd.
Printed in the Holy Land, 1998

A WALK WITH JESUS IN THE HOLY LAND

This book is a unique and spectacular photographic album featuring the places Jesus lived, journeyed, visited, and took action–from Nazareth to Jerusalem via Bethlehem, Galilee, and the Sea of Galilee. It is a photographic pathway through the holy sites connected to all of the most crucial junctures of Jesus' life and death, from the Annunciation to the Pentecost.

This volume's distinctiveness lies in its presentation of the holy sites at the peak of their glory, on the pilgrimage days of the most important annual ceremonies. At these moments, these spots, full of pilgrims, praying crowds, and members of the clergy wearing their splendid vestments, are intensely evocative. Participate in the ceremony of the Annunciation in Nazareth and the Midnight Mass in the Church of the Nativity in Bethlehem; ascend to the Quarantel Monastery in a line of pilgrims, sit on the stone seat where Jesus fasted for forty days, and stand opposite the devil on the Pinnacle of the temple.

Experience the church at Cana on the day of the commemoration of Jesus' first miracle. Pray in the glow of the candles illuminating the Church of the Loaves and Fishes in Tabgha on pilgrimage day. Sail to Jesus' city on the Sea of Galilee and walk among the ruins of ancient synagogues in the towns he cursed. Listen once more to the words he spoke on the Mount of Beatitudes, then visit Mount Tabor, Bethphage, and Bethany. Attend the Church of Dominus Flevit during the commemoration of Jesus' weeping for Jerusalem. Take part in the foot-washing and Holy Fire ceremonies at the Church of the Holy Sepulcher during Holy Week. Travel the Via Dolorosa, visiting each of the fourteen stations, and finally, feel your spirits rise at the Church of Emmaus.

This beautiful book takes you on a pilgrimage to the Holy Land, following in the footsteps of Jesus in all his glory. It walks with you in the lanes Jesus passed through two thousand years ago. You will catch your breath opposite the Mount of the Precipice, hear the lapping of the waves of the Sea of Galilee, wipe tears from your eyes before the Rock of Agony, and feel your legs buckle on the Via Dolorosa.

All photographs are accompanied by the appropriate verses from the New Testament. At the end of the volume is an index of explanations regarding every site and ceremony.

◇ **The ceremony of the Annunciation of the Lord in the Basilica of the Annunciation in Nazareth.**

◁ "God sent the angel Gabriel to Nazareth . . ." (Luke 26:1). ◇ **The Basilica of the Annunciation in Nazareth.**

◇ In the crypt of the Basilica of the Annunciation during the ceremony of the Annunciation of the Lord.

"In the sixth month, God sent the angel Gabriel to Nazareth, a town in Galilee, to a virgin pledged to be married to a man named Joseph, a descendant of David. The virgin's name was Mary. The angel went to her and said, 'Greetings, you who are highly favored! The Lord is with you.' Mary was greatly distressed at his words and wondered what kind of greeting this might be. But the angel said to her, 'Have no fear, Mary, you have found favor with God. You will be with child and give birth to a son, and you are to give him the name Jesus. He will be great and will be called the Son of the Most High. The Lord God will grant him the throne of his father David, and he will reign over the house of Jacob forever; his kingdom will never end.'" (Luke 1:26-33)

"'Greetings, you who are highly favored! The Lord is with you'" (Luke 1:28).
◇ **Mary's Well on the day of the commemoration of the Annunciation in the Greek Orthodox Church of the Annunciation.**

◇ Mary's Well

◇ The ceremony in remembrance of the Annunciation.

"Then Mary got ready and hurried to a town in the hill country of Judea . . ." (Luke 1:39). ◇ **The Church of the Visitation in Ein Karem.**

"She entered Zechariah's home and greeted Elizabeth" (Luke 1:40). ◇ **In front of the Church of the Visitation.** ▷

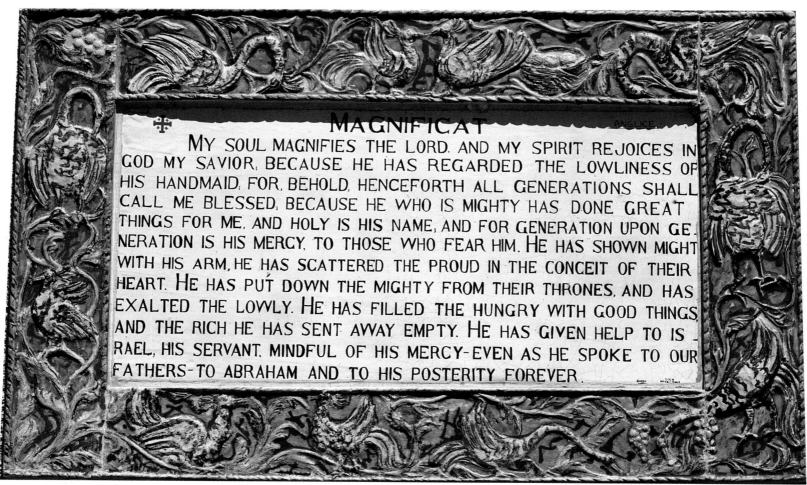

◇ **A wall in the courtyard of the Church of the Visitation on which the Magnificat is written in forty-one different languages.**

"'Blessed are you among women, and blessed is the child you will bear!'" (Luke 1:42). ◇ **The Visitation of Mary to Elizabeth. The ceremony on the day** ▷
of pilgrimage to the Church of the Visitation.

"While they were there, the time came for the baby to be born" (Luke 2:6).
◇ **Midnight Mass in the Church of Saint Catherine in the Church of the Nativity in Bethlehem.**

"So Joseph also went up from the town of Nazareth in Galilee to Judea, to Bethlehem the town of David" (Luke 2:4).
◁ ◇ **The procession of the Patriarch's entrance into the Church of the Nativity in Bethlehem.**

"[A]nd she gave birth to her firstborn, a son. She wrapped him in cloths and placed him in a manger" (Luke 2:7).
◇ **Midnight Mass in the Church of Saint Catherine.**

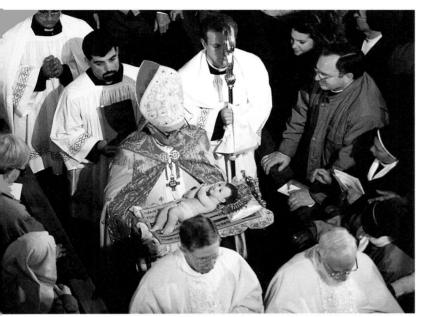

◇ The Patriarch carries the Child of Bethlehem.

◇ The southern entrance of the Grotto of the Nativity.

◇ Women light candles next to the manger.

◇ The silver star that marks Jesus' birthplace.

"And there were shepherds living in the nearby fields . . ." (Luke 2:8). ◇ **The Shepherds' Field in Beit Sahur, east of Bethlehem.**

◇ **Shepherds' Field Church.** ▷

"Do not be afraid. I bring you good news of great joy that will be for all the people. Today in the town of David a Savior has been born to you; he is Christ the Lord. This will be a sign to you: You will find a baby wrapped in cloths and lying in a manger." **(Luke 2:10-12)**

"'Today in the town of David a Savior has been born to you; he is Christ the Lord'" (Luke 2:11).

"So they hurried off and found Mary and Joseph, and the baby, who was lying in the manger" (Luke 2:16).
◇ **Frescoes in the Shepherds' Field Church.**

◇ **The entrance to the Milk Grotto in Bethlehem.** ▷

"'Get up,' he said, 'take the child and his mother and escape to Egypt'" (Matthew 2:13). ◇ **The way to Egypt.**

◁ "Magi came to Jerusalem from the east and asked, 'Where is the one who has been born king of the Jews? We saw his star in the east and have
32 come to worship him'" (Matthew 2:1-2). ◇ **The altar in the Milk Grotto.**

"And he went and lived in a town called Nazareth" (Matthew 2:23).

◇ **The Holy Family: a sculpture at the Church of Saint Joseph in Nazareth.**

◇ **A Catholic baptism in the Jordan River at the baptism site near Jericho.**

◁ "When all the people were being baptized, Jesus was baptized too. And as he was praying, heaven was opened . . ." (Luke 3:21).

◇ **The pilgrimage to the Jordan River on the anniversary of Jesus' baptism. The ceremony in the Franciscan chapel.**

◇ Greek Orthodox pilgrims on their way to be baptized in the Jordan River.

◇ A Greek Orthodox baptism at the baptism site near Jericho.

"A voice of one calling in the desert, 'Make ready the way for the Lord, make straight paths for him'" (Mark 1:3).

"Then Jesus was led by the Spirit into the desert to be tempted by the devil" (Matthew 4:1). ◇ **The Quarantel Monastery in the Judean Desert.**

"For forty days he was tempted by the devil" (Luke 4:2). ◇ **The stone seat in the Chapel of the Temptation in the Quarantel Monastery.**

"The devil led him to Jerusalem and had him stand on the highest point of the temple" (Luke 4:9). ◇ **The Pinnacle of the temple.** ▷

"If you are the Son of God, cast yourself down from here. For it is written: He will command his angels regarding you to protect you carefully; they will lift you up in their hands, so that you will not strike your foot against a stone."

"It says: Do not put the Lord your God to the test." *(Luke 4:9-12)*

"He went and lived in Capernaum, which was by the lake . . ." (Matthew 4:13). ◇ **A bird's-eye view of Capernaum.**

◁ "They . . . took him to the brow of the hill on which the town was built, in order to cast him down from the cliff" (Luke 4:29).
◇ **The Mount of the Precipice near Nazareth.**

"As Jesus was walking beside the Sea of Galilee, he saw two brothers . . ." (Matthew 4:18).
◇ **A view of the Valley of Beit Saida from the Sea of Galilee.**

"'Follow me,' Jesus said, 'and I will make you fishers of men'" (Matthew 4:19). ◇ **A fisherman on the Sea of Galilee.**

"On the third day a wedding occurred at Cana in Galilee" (John 2:1). ◇ **The Churches of the Miracle at Cana: *(right)* the Greek Orthodox Church of Nathanael (Saint Bartholomew) and *(left)* the Franciscan church.**

◇ The gables of the Franciscan Church of the Miracle.

◇ Pilgrimage to Cana.

◇ The water jar in the crypt of the Franciscan Church of the Miracle.

◇ The ceremony in memory of Jesus' first miracle.

"One day Jesus was standing by the Lake of Gennesaret, with the people crowding around him and listening to the word of God . . ." (Luke 5:1).
◇ **An aerial photograph of Lake Ginnosar (the Sea of Galilee) and the Ginnosar Valley.**

Blessed are the poor in spirit, for theirs is the kingdom of heaven.
Blessed are those who mourn, for they will be comforted.
Blessed are the meek, for they will inherit the earth.
Blessed are those who hunger and thirst for righteousness, for they will be filled.
Blessed are the merciful, for they will be shown mercy.
Blessed are the pure in heart, for they will see God.
Blessed are the peacemakers, for they will be called sons of God.
Blessed are those who are persecuted because of righteousness, for theirs is the kingdom of heaven.
Blessed are you when people insult you, persecute you and falsely say all kinds of evil against you because of me.

(Matthew 5:3-11)

◇ **The Mount of Beatitudes.**

"Soon afterwards, Jesus went to a town called Nain . . ." (Luke 7:11).
◇ **The church at Nain, where Jesus performed the miracle of the raising of a widow's son.**

◇ **A storm on the Sea of Galilee.** ▷

"Without warning, a furious storm arose on the lake, so that the waves swept over the boat. But Jesus was sleeping. The disciples went and woke him, saying, 'Lord, save us! We are going to drown!'
He replied, 'You of little faith, why are you so afraid?' Then he got up and rebuked the winds and the waves, and it was completely calm.
Then men were amazed and asked, 'What kind of man is this? Even the winds and the waves obey him!'" (Matthew 8:23-27)

"The herd, about two thousand in number, rushed down the steep slope into the lake and were drowned" (Mark 5:13).
◇ **The church at Kursi.**

◁ "When Jesus stepped ashore, he was met by a demon-possessed man from the town" (Luke 8:27).
◇ **The sacred rock and the ruins of the ancient chapel at Kursi.**

"Jesus stepped into a boat, crossed over and came into his own town" (Matthew 9:1).
◇ **A view of Capernaum from the Sea of Galilee.**

"'Woe to you, Korazin!'" (Matthew 11:21). ◇ **The ancient synagogue at Korazin in Galilee.**

"'And you, Capernaum, will you be lifted up to the skies? No, you will descend to the depths'" (Matthew 11:23).
◇ **The ancient synagogue at Capernaum.**

"Jacob's well was there, and Jesus, tired as he was from the journey, sat down by the well" (John 4:6).
◇ **Jacob's Well near the city of Nablus.**

"Taking the five loaves and the two fish . . . They all ate and were satisfied . . ." (Matthew 14:19-20).
◇ **The ceremony commemorating the multiplication of the loaves and fishes at the Church of the Loaves and Fishes at Tabgha.** ▷

◇ **Pilgrims next to the Church of the Loaves and Fishes on the pilgrimage day.**

◇ The ceremony in the Church of the Loaves and Fishes.

◇ A mosaic of the loaves and fishes in the Church of the Loaves and Fishes at Tabgha.

"Jesus . . . went . . . down to the Sea of Galilee and into the territory of the Decapolis" (Mark 7:31).
◇ **The border of the city of Susita, one of the ten cities of the Decapolis.**

"[H]e got into the boat with his disciples and sailed to the region of Dalmanutha" (Mark 8:10). ◇ **Dalmanutha.** ▷

"Jesus and his disciples went on to the villages around Caesarea Philippi" (Mark 8:27).
◇ **The ruins of the church in Caesarea Philippi near Banias.**

"If anyone would come after me, he must deny himself and take up his cross and follow me. For whoever wants to save his life will lose it, but whoever loses his life for me and for the gospel will save it." (Mark 8:34-35)

"Six days later, Jesus took with him Peter, James and John the brother of James . . ." (Matthew 17:1).

◇ **The way to the summit of Mount Tabor. An aerial photograph from the west.** ▷

"[A]nd led them up a high mountain by themselves" (Matthew 17:1). ◇ **The monasteries on Mount Tabor.**

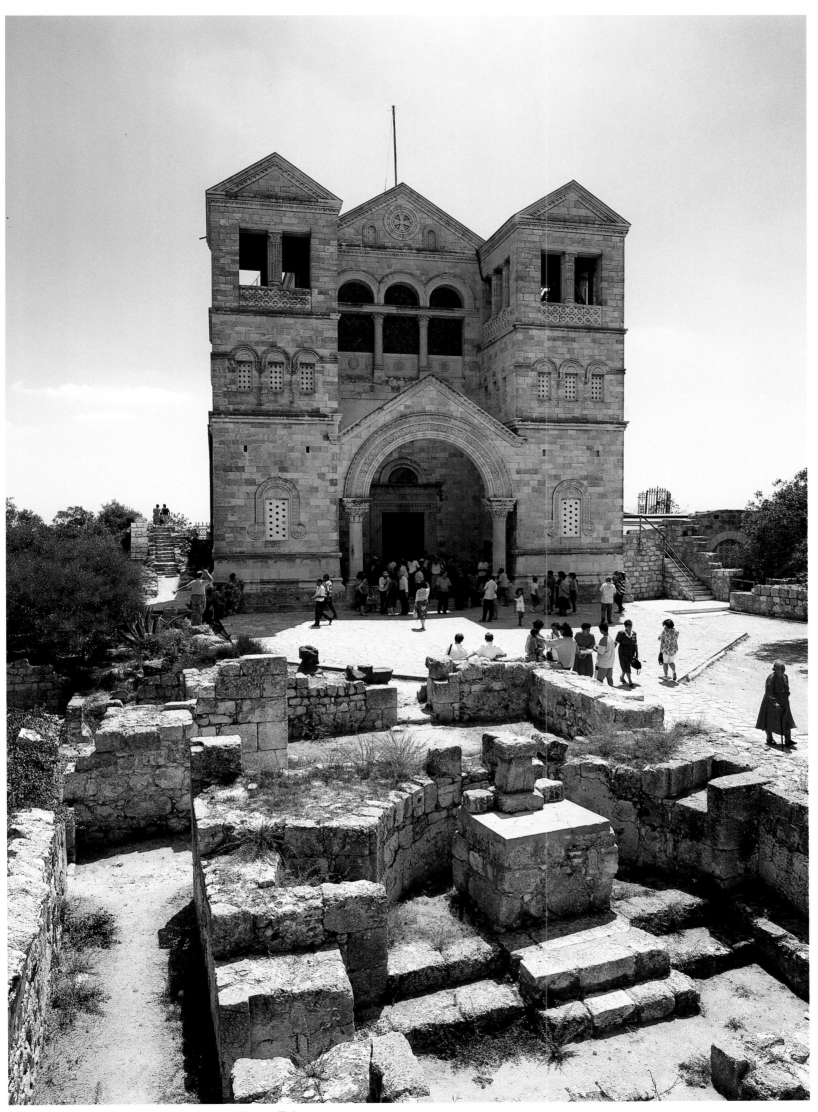

◇ The Basilica of the Transfiguration on Mount Tabor.

65

"There he was transfigured before them. His face shone like the sun, and his clothes became as white as the light" (Matthew 17:2).

◇ **The ceremony commemorating the Transfiguration of the Lord in the Basilica of the Transfiguration.**

"Just then there appeared before them Moses and Elijah, conversing with Jesus" (Matthew 17:3).

◇ **The apse of the Basilica of the Transfiguration.**

"Jesus entered Jericho and was passing through" (Luke 19:1).
◇ **The city of Jericho from the direction of the Quarantel Monastery.**

"A man by the name of Zacchaeus was there . . . he ran ahead and climbed a sycamore-fig tree to see him . . ." (Luke 19:2-4).
◇ **A sycamore-fig tree.**

◇ The village of Bethany.

"As Jesus and his disciples were on their way, he came to a village where a woman named Martha opened her home to him" (Luke 10:38).
◇ **Jesus in the house of Martha and Mary: a mosaic in the Church of Lazarus in Bethany.**

"Lord, don't you care that my sister has left me to do the
work by myself? Tell her to help me!"
"Martha, Martha, you are worried and distressed about
many things, but only one thing is needed.
Mary has chosen what is better, and it will not be taken away
from her." (Luke 10:40-42)

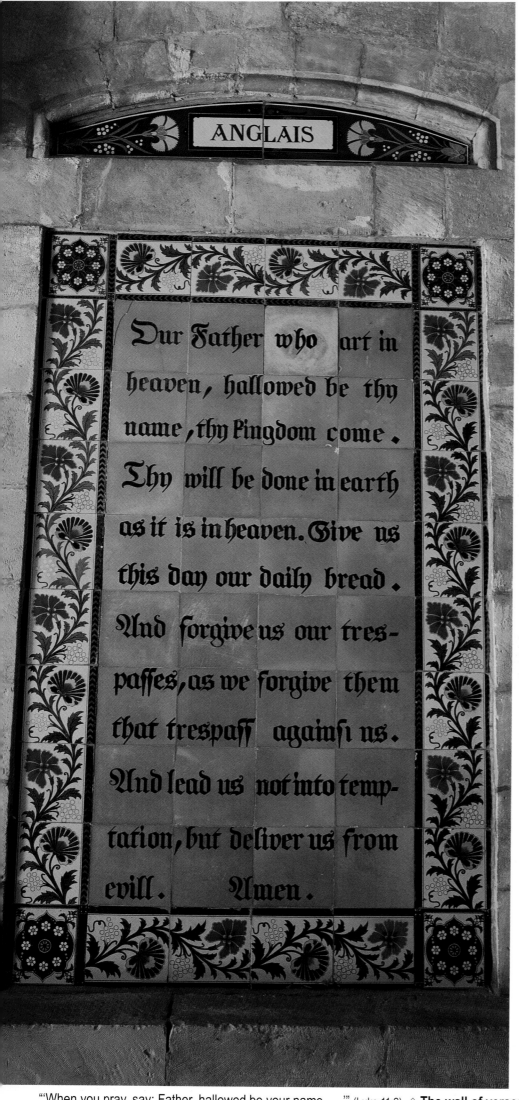

ANGLAIS

Our Father who art in heaven, hallowed be thy name, thy kingdom come. Thy will be done in earth as it is in heaven. Give us this day our daily bread. And forgive us our trespasses, as we forgive them that trespass against us. And lead us not into temptation, but deliver us from evill. Amen.

"'When you pray, say: Father, hallowed be your name . . .'" (Luke 11:2). ◇ **The wall of verses at the Eleona (the Church of the Pater Noster).**

SUÈDOIS

Fader wår som åst i
himmelen, helgat warde
titt nampn, tillkomme titt
ricke. Skee tin wilie så på
iordenne som i himmelen.
Giff oss i dagh wårt dagligs
bröd. Och förlåt oß wåra
skulder så som ock wi för-
låton them oß skyldige
åro. Och inledh oß icke
i frestelse, uthan fräls oß
i frå ondo.   Amen.

GEORGIEN

MĄMAO ciweno romeli
char zatha scina, tzminda
igawn sachsli sceni; mowe-
din supeka sceni. Igaw neba
sceni witharza zatha sci-
na eghre kneganisa zeela.
Puri ciweni arsobisa mo-
mez ciwensdghes . Da
momitewen ciwenthanā nā-
debni ciweni witharzā ci-
wen miutewetthana mdeb-
tha math ciwentha. Da
nan sceniuganeb ciwen
gansazdelza; aramed mi-
chsen ciwen borotisagan.
        Amin.

POLONAIS

Ojca nasz, ktoryś
jest w niebiesiech,
swieć sie imieTwoje,
przyidz Krolestwo Two
bądz wola Twoja
jako w niebie tak i na
ziemi. Chleba nasze-
go powszedniego day
nam dzisiaj i odpuść
nam nasze winy, jako
i my odpuszczamy na
szym winowajcom, i
nie wwódz nas na
pokuszenie, ale nas
zbaw ode złego.
        Amen.

"'Go,' he told him, 'bathe in the Pool of Siloam . . .'" (John 9:7). ◇ **The Pool of Siloam in Jerusalem.**

"'Lazarus is dead . . . let us go to him'" (John 11:14-15). ◇ **The Church of Lazarus in Bethany**.

"'I am the resurrection and the life. He who believes in me will live, though he dies'" (John 11:25).
◇ **The pilgrimage to Bethany. The Greek Orthodox ceremony next to the tomb of Lazarus.**

"'Lazarus, come out!'" (John 11:43). ◇ **The tomb of Lazarus in Bethany.**

◁ "When Mary reached the place where Jesus was and saw him, she fell at his feet . . ." (John 11:32). ◇ **The altar in the Church of Lazarus.**

"As they approached Jerusalem and came to Bethphage on the Mount of Olives . . ." (Matthew 21:1). ◇ **The church at Bethphage.**

"'See, your king comes to you, gentle and riding on a donkey, on a colt, the foal of a donkey'" (Matthew 21:5).
◇ **The pilgrimage to Bethphage on the day before Palm Sunday.**

◇ The Greek Orthodox Patriarch.

◇ The Armenian Palm Sunday mass.

◇ The Coptic Patriarch.

◇ At the Palm Sunday mass.

◇ **Palm Sunday mass in the Church of the Holy Sepulcher.**
◁ "They brought the donkey and the colt, placed their cloaks on them, and Jesus sat on them" (Matthew 21:7). ◇ **The Latin Patriarch.**

"They took palm branches and went out to meet him . . ." (John 12:13). ◇ **The commemoration of the Lord in Bethphage on Palm Sunday.**

"Those who went ahead and those who followed shouted, 'Hosanna! Blessed is he who comes in the name of the Lord!'" (Mark 11:9).

◇ **The Palm Sunday procession.** ▷

"As he approached Jerusalem and saw the city, he wept over it . . ." (Luke 19:41).
◇ **The Church of Dominus Flevit on the Mount of Olives in Jerusalem.**

◁   ◇ **The Palm Sunday procession on the Mount of Olives.**

"'If you, even you, had only known on this day what would bring you peace—but now it is hidden from your eyes'" (Luke 19:42).
◇ **The commemoration of the weeping of the Lord at the Church of Dominus Flevit.**

"'O Jerusalem, Jerusalem . . . how often have I longed to gather your children together as a hen gathers her chicks under her wings'" (Matthew 23:37).
◇ **The pilgrimage to the Church of Dominus Flevit**.

"When Jesus entered Jerusalem, the whole city was stirred . . ." (Matthew 21:10).
◇ **The entrance to Jerusalem via the Lions' Gate during the Palm Sunday procession.**

◁ ◇ **The Palm Sunday procession on the slope of the Mount of Olives.**

◇ **Female pilgrims dressed as brides in the Palm Sunday procession.**

"At that time the kingdom of heaven will be like ten virgins who took their lamps and went out to meet the bridegroom. Five of them were foolish and five were wise. The foolish ones took their lamps but did not take oil with them. The wise, however, took oil in jars along with their lamps.
The bridegroom was a long time in coming, and they all became drowsy and fell asleep. At midnight the cry rang out: 'Here's the bridegroom! Come out to meet him!'
All the virgins awoke and trimmed their lamps. The foolish ones said to the wise, 'Give us some of your oil; our lamps are going out.'
'No,' they replied, 'there may not be enough for both us and you. Instead, go to those who sell oil and buy some for yourselves.'
But while they were on their way to buy the oil, the bridegroom arrived. The virgins who were ready went in with him to the wedding banquet. And the door was shut."

(Matthew 25:1-10)

"The crowds replied, 'This is Jesus, the prophet from Nazareth in Galilee'" (Matthew 21:11).
◇ **The concluding ceremony of the Palm Sunday procession at Saint Anne's Church in Jerusalem.**

"'Do you see all these grand buildings?' replied Jesus, 'Not one stone here will be left on another; every one will be thrown down'" (Mark 13:2).
◇ **The ruins of the Temple Mount.**

"Jesus entered the temple area and drove out all who were buying and selling there" (Matthew 21:12).
◁ ◇ **The steps leading to the Hulda Gates at the entrance to the ancient temple.**

93

"'Where is the lodging, where I may eat the Passover with my disciples?'" (Luke 22:11). ◇ **The Church of the Dormition** *(at bottom)* **and the building of the Tomb of King David and the Cenacle** *(at top)* **in an aerial photograph of the summit of Mount Zion.**

◁ "As Jesus was sitting on the Mount of Olives opposite the temple . . ." (Mark 13:3). ◇ **The Mount of Olives.**

"When evening came, Jesus arrived with the Twelve. While they were reclining at the table eating, he said, 'I tell you truly, one of you will betray me—one who is eating with me'" (Mark 14:17). ◇ **The pilgrimage to the Cenacle on Holy Thursday.**

"After that, he poured water into a basin and began to wash his disciples' feet, drying them with the towel that was wrapped around him" (John 13:5).

◇ **The Greek Orthodox foot-washing ceremony in the courtyard in front of the Church of the Holy Sepulcher.** ▷

"'Unless I wash you, you have no part with me'" (John 13:8).
◇ **The Catholic foot-washing ceremony in the Church of the Holy Sepulcher.**

◇ A pilgrim watches the Greek Orthodox foot-washing ceremony.

◇ The Armenian foot-washing ceremony in Saint James' Church.

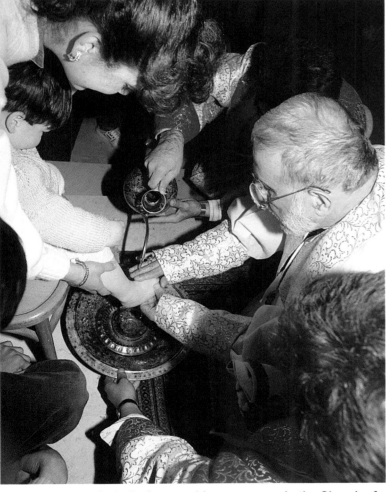

◇ The Armenian Catholic foot-washing ceremony in the Church of Our Lady of the Spasm.

◇ The Ethiopian foot-washing ceremony in the Deir el-Sultan.

"'Now that I, your Lord and Teacher, have washed your feet, you also should wash one another's feet. I have set you an example so that you should do ▷ as I have done for you'" (John 13:14-15). ◇ **The Greek Orthodox foot-washing ceremony.**

"Jesus left with his disciples and crossed the Kidron Valley" (John 18:1).

◇ **The Scala Santa (Sacred Stairway) that leads from Mount Zion to the Kidron Valley.**

"On the other side was an olive grove, and he and his disciples entered it" (John 18:1).

◇ **The olive grove of Gethsemane.**

103

"'My soul is overwhelmed with sorrow to the point of death. Stay here and watch with me'" (Matthew 26:38).
◇ **The Church of All Nations (Basilica of the Agony) in Gethsemane.**

◁ "They went to a place called Gethsemane, and Jesus said to his disciples, 'Sit here while I pray'" (Mark 14:32).

◇ **The Grotto of Gethsemane.**

"'My Father, if it is possible, may this cup be taken from me. Yet not as I will, but as you will'" (Matthew 26:39).
◇ Holy Hour in the Church of All Nations at Gethsemane.

"'Judas, are you betraying the Son of Man with a kiss?'" (Luke 22:48).
◇ **The Pillar of the Kiss in Gethsemane.**

"'The man I kiss is the man; arrest him'" (Matthew 26:48).
◇ **A mosaic of Judas' kiss in the Church of All Nations.**

◁ ◇ **The Rock of Agony.**

"Those who had arrested Jesus took him to Caiaphas, the high priest, where the teachers of the law and the elders had gathered" (Matthew 26:57).
◇ **The Church of Saint Peter in Gallicantu, built over the traditional site of the house of the high priest Caiaphas.**

◇ The ossuary of the high priest Caiaphas.

◇ Christ's prison in the Church of Saint Peter in Gallicantu.

"They bound him, led him away . . ." (Matthew 27:2).
◇ **The Prison of Christ in the Greek church along the Via Dolorosa.**

"[A]nd handed him over to Pilate, the governor" (Matthew 27:2). ◇ **The Antonia Fortress: a view from the direction of the Temple Mount.** ◇

*"We have found this man subverting our
nation. He opposes payment of taxes to
Caesar and claims to be Christ, a king."*
"Are you the king of the Jews?"
"Yes, it is as you say."
"I find no basis for a charge against this man."

(Luke 23:2-4)

"Pilate said to them, 'Here is the man!'" (John 19:5). ◇ **The Ecce Homo Arch in the Ecce Homo Chapel.**

◁ "Then Pilate took Jesus and had him flogged. The soldiers twisted together a crown of thorns and set it on his head" (John 19:1-2).
◇ **The Church of the Flagellation.**

117

"When Pilate heard this, he brought Jesus out and sat down on the judge's seat at a place known as the Stone Pavement . . ." (John 19:13).

◇ **The pilgrimage to the Lithostrotos in Jerusalem.**

◇ **Prayer at the Lithostrotos on the pilgrimage day.**

"When Pilate saw that he was getting nowhere . . . he took water and washed his hands . . . 'I am innocent of this man's blood,' he said" (Matthew 27:24).
◇ **"Pontius Pilate," an inscription carved in a stone in Caesarea.**

The Way of the Cross
on the
Via Dolorosa

"Finally Pilate handed him over to them to be crucified" (John 19:16).

◇ Station **I.** Jesus is condemned to death. The courtyard of the Antonia Fortress (today the courtyard of Omariye College).

122

"But he had Jesus flogged, and turned him over to be crucified" (Matthew 27:26).
◇ **Station II. Jesus takes up the cross. The Chapel of the Condemnation.**

◇ **Jesus falls under the cross for the first time. The Catholic Procession of the Cross at Station III.** ▷

◇ Station **IV**. Jesus is met by his mother.

"As they were leaving, they met a man from Cyrene named Simon, and they forced him to carry the cross" (Matthew 27:32).
◇ **Simon of Cyrene helps Jesus carry the cross. The Greek Orthodox Procession of the Cross at Station V.**

◇ The interior of the Franciscan chapel at Station V.

◇ **Station VI. Veronica wipes the sweat from Jesus' face.**

◇ **Station VII. Jesus falls for the second time.** ▷

◇ **Station VIII. Jesus consoles the women of Jerusalem.**

"Daughters of Jerusalem, do not weep for me; weep for yourselves and your children. For the time will come when you will say, 'Blessed are the barren women, the wombs that never bore and the breasts that never nursed!' Then they will say to the mountains, 'Fall on us!' and to the hills, 'Cover us!'" (Luke 23:28-30)

◇ Station IX. Jesus falls for the third time.

◇ An aerial photograph of the Church of the Holy Sepulcher.

◇ The Catholic Procession of the Cross in the Atrium of the Church of the Holy Sepulcher. ▷

◇ **A pilgrim kisses a pillar at the entrance to the Church of the Holy Sepulcher.**

◇ The Greek Orthodox Procession of the Cross in the Atrium of the Church of the Holy Sepulcher.

◇ The Greek Orthodox Procession of the Cross, before entering the Church of the Holy Sepulcher. ▷ 135

◇ **Christ's Prison Chapel in the Church of the Holy Sepulcher.**

◇ Station X. Jesus is stripped of his garments.

"It was the third hour when they crucified him" (Mark 15:25). ◇ **Station XI. Jesus is nailed to the cross. The Altar of the Crucifixion.**

"Carrying his own cross, he went out to the Place of the Skull (which in Aramaic is called Golgotha). Here they crucified him, and with him two others–one on each side and Jesus in the middle. Pilate had a notice prepared and fastened to the cross. It read: JESUS OF NAZARETH, KING OF THE JEWS."

(John 19:17-19)

"And at the ninth hour Jesus cried out in a loud voice, 'Eloi, Eloi, lama sabachthani . . .'" (Mark 15:34). ◇ **The Altar of the Cross at Station XII.**

"'Father, into your hands I commit my spirit'" (Luke 23:46). ◇ **Station XII. Jesus dies on the cross.** ▷ 141

"Near Jesus' cross stood his mother, his mother's sister, Mary the wife of Clopas, and Mary Magdalene" (John 19:25).
◇ **The Place of the Three Women.**

◇ **Station XIII. Jesus is taken down from the cross. The Altar of Our Lady of Sorrows (Mater Dolorosa).**

"He was accompanied by Nicodemus . . . [who] brought a mixture of myrrh and aloes, about seventy-five pounds" (John 19:39).
◇ **The Stone of the Anointing in the Church of the Holy Sepulcher.**

"Taking Jesus' body, the two of them wrapped it with the spices in strips of linen, in accordance with Jewish burial custom" (John 19:40).
◇ **Around the Stone of the Anointing.**

"[A]nd placed it in his own new tomb that he had hewn out of the rock. He rolled a big stone in front of the entrance to the tomb . . ." (Matthew 27:60).
◇ **The rotunda and aedicule of the Holy Tomb.**

◇ **Station XIV. Jesus is laid in the tomb. The aedicule of the Holy Tomb.** ▷

◇ The entrance to the aedicule of the Holy Tomb.

◇ The Chapel of the Angel–the anteroom of the Tomb of Christ. ▷

◇ **The Tomb of Christ.**

"The next day, the one after Preparation Day, the chief priests and the Pharisees went to Pilate. 'Sir,' they said, 'we remember that while he was still alive that deceiver said, 'After three days I will rise again.' So give the order for the tomb to be made secure until the third day. Otherwise, his disciples might come and steal the body and tell the people that he has risen from the dead. This last deception will be worse than the first.' 'Take a guard,' Pilate answered, 'Go, make the tomb as secure as you know how.' So they went and made the tomb secure by putting a seal on the stone and posting the guard." (Matthew 27:62-66)

◇ **On the threshold of the Holy Tomb.**

◁ "At the place Jesus was crucified, there was a garden, and in the garden was a new tomb . . ." (John 19:41).

◇ **The Garden Tomb in Jerusalem**.

◇ The Catholic Ceremony of the Holy Fire in the vestibule of the Church of the Holy Sepulcher.

"After the Sabbath, at dawn on the first day of the week, Mary Magdalene and the other Mary went to look at the tomb. There was a violent earthquake, for an angel of the Lord came down from heaven and, going to the tomb, rolled back the stone and sat on it. His appearance was like lightning, and his clothes were as white as snow." *(Matthew 28:1-3)*

◇ Lighting the fire in the rotunda of the Church of the Holy Sepulcher during the Greek Orthodox Ceremony of the Holy Fire. ▷   157

◇ **Bringing the Holy Fire into the Atrium.**

◇ **The Holy Fire passes among the devout.** ▷

"When he was at the table with them, he took bread, gave thanks, broke it and began to give it to them" (Luke 24:30).
◇ **The ceremony in the Church of Emmaus in El-Qubeibeh during the pilgrimage on Easter Monday.**

◁ "Now that same day two of them were going to a village called Emmaus . . . Jesus himself came up and walked along with them . . ." (Luke 24:13-15).
◇ **The Church of Emmaus in El-Qubeibeh.**

◇ **The ceremony in the ancient church in Emmaus in the Ajalon Valley during the pilgrimage on Easter Monday.** ▷ 163

"Afterwards Jesus appeared again to his disciples by the Sea of Tiberias" (John 21:1).
◇ **Prayer in the courtyard of the Church of the Primacy of Peter at Tabgha.**

"Early in the morning, Jesus stood on the shore . . ." (John 21:4). ◇ **The Church of the Primacy of Peter.** ▷

"When they landed, they saw a fire of burning coals there with fish on it, and some bread" (John 21:9).
◇ **The Mensa Christi (Table of the Lord) in the Church of the Primacy of Peter.**

"Simon, son of John, do you truly love me more than these?"
"Yes, Lord, you know that I love you."
"Feed my lambs."
(John 21:15)

◇ **The statue depicting the primacy of Peter at Tabgha.**

"After the Lord Jesus had spoken to them, he was taken up into heaven and he sat at the right hand of God" (Mark 16:19).
◇ **The Chapel of the Ascension on the pilgrimage day of the Eastern Orthodox churches.**

◁ "When he had led them out to the vicinity of Bethany, he lifted up his hands and blessed them" (Luke 24:50).
◇ **An aerial photograph of the Chapel of the Ascension on the Mount of Olives.**

◇ Jesus' footprint in the rock from which he ascended to heaven, in the Chapel of the Ascension.

◇ The Armenian ceremony in the Chapel of the Ascension.

◇ Pilgrimage to the Cenacle.

◇ Pentecost. The mass in the Church of the Dormition. ▷

◇ **A fountain in the cloister of the Church of the Loaves and Fishes in Tabgha.**

"Therefore everyone who hears these words of mine and puts them into practice is like a wise man who built his house on the rock. The rain descended, the streams rose, and the winds blew and beat against that house; yet it did not fall, because it had its foundations on the rock."

(Matthew 7:24-25)

BEHIND THE PHOTOGRAPHS

1 ◇ **Easter Eggs**
Easter eggs covered with colored beads in imitation of Russian Easter eggs are sold in the bazaar of Jerusalem's Old City.

2-3 ◇ **The Milk Grotto in Bethlehem**
See 29-30.

4-5 ◇ **The Palm Sunday Procession**
See 82-84.

6-7 ◇ **The Commemoration of the Weeping of the Lord in the Church of Dominus Flevit**
See 85-87.

8-9 ◇ **A Detail on the Facade of the Holy Tomb**
See 148-154.

10 ◇ **The Opening of the Doors to the Church of the Holy Sepulcher**
Ever since the fall of the Crusader kingdom, Muslims have held the keys to the Church of the Holy Sepulcher. Even today the doors of the church are opened by one of the members of the Nusseibeh family. Here, Wajeeh Nusseibeh climbs a ladder to open the two round locks with the ancient key.

12-14 ◇ **The Basilica of the Annunciation in Nazareth**
The Basilica of the Annunciation is one of the largest and most magnificent churches in the Middle East. Designed by the Italian architect Giovanni Muzio, it was consecrated in 1969.

In the fifth century, a Byzantine church with an expansive nave, a courtyard with a portico, and a small monastery to its south was established on this spot. A flight of stairs led from the church's northern wing to the Grotto of the Annunciation, which was not connected to the church. The date of the destruction of the church is unknown. The Crusaders began building a majestic basilica similar in plan to its predecessor, but the apparently unfinished building was destroyed by the Muslims. In the seventeenth century, the Franciscans erected a modest church and monastery on the site. The former was renovated, enlarged, and its facade rebuilt in 1877, but was later destroyed to make way for the current church.

The current church was built on two levels in order to allow for the incorporation of the ancient remains. Its western facade is designed in the shape of a pyramid, at the peak of which stands a statue of Jesus. On the upper portion of the facade are carved the figures of Mary and the angel Gabriel, with the figures of the four Evangelists below them. The three splendid doors are made of copper with bronze panels depicting various events from Jesus' life.

The upper church is impressive in size. Its high dome, which was fashioned in the shape of a Madonna lily, is almost the sole source of light in the church. It opens out towards the rock that houses the grotto, and symbolizes the Holy Spirit's descent to Mary. The floor is decorated with a tessellated marble design in which are integrated the names of popes who expressed admiration for Mary. Lovely mosaics adorn the apses and walls of the nave.

15-17 ◇ The Church of Saint Gabriel in Nazareth

The Church of Saint Gabriel in Nazareth is the Greek Orthodox Church of the Annunciation. According to Greek Orthodox tradition, the angel Gabriel announced the birth of Jesus to Mary as she was going to draw water from a spring here. The first church on the site was built by the Crusaders above the spring in the early twelfth century, and destroyed in 1263. The present church, which was built in 1750, incorporates the remains of the Crusader church's crypt. In the crypt is Mary's Well, next to which Mary stood during the Annunciation.

18-21 ◇ The Church of the Visitation in Ein Karem

The Church of the Visitation is apparently the more ancient of the two churches in Ein Karem. Tradition attributes its construction to Empress Helena, Constantine's mother, who identified the site as the home of Zechariah and the place where he and Elizabeth hid from Herod's soldiers. The Crusaders later identified the site as the place where the meeting between Elizabeth and Mary took place and erected a two-story church on the ruins of the ancient church.

When the Crusaders left the Holy Land, the church fell into Muslim hands and gradually deteriorated. The Franciscans purchased the building in 1679, but only in 1862 was the lower level of the church restored. Work on the upper level of the structure began in 1938, and was completed in 1955. Within the current church, designed by the architect Antonio Barluzzi, the ancient remains are preserved.

The lower church has frescoes depicting the Visitation, Elizabeth hiding her son John, and Zechariah next to the altar in the temple. An ancient cistern from which Zechariah and Elizabeth drank is also to be found in the church; according to tradition, the stone next to it hid the two from Herod's soldiers.

The upper hall is dedicated to Mary, and its walls are decorated with paintings in honor of her. Verses from the Magnificat are engraved on the columns of the church, and on the wall opposite it are forty-two ceramic tablets bearing verses from the Magnificat in forty-two different languages. On the church's facade is a striking mosaic commemorating the Visitation.

22-25 ◇ The Church of the Nativity in Bethlehem

"So Joseph also went up from the town of Nazareth in Galilee to Judea, to Bethlehem the town of David, because he belonged to the house and line of David. He went there to register with Mary, who was pledged to be married to him and was expecting a child. While they were there, the time came for the baby to be born, and she gave birth to her firstborn, a son. She wrapped him in cloths and placed him in a manger, because there was no room for them in the inn" (Luke 2:4-7).

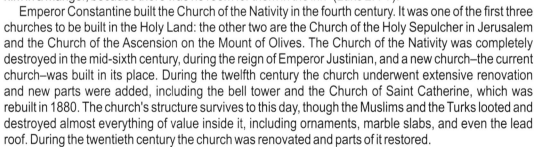

Emperor Constantine built the Church of the Nativity in the fourth century. It was one of the first three churches to be built in the Holy Land: the other two are the Church of the Holy Sepulcher in Jerusalem and the Church of the Ascension on the Mount of Olives. The Church of the Nativity was completely destroyed in the mid-sixth century, during the reign of Emperor Justinian, and a new church–the current church–was built in its place. During the twelfth century the church underwent extensive renovation and new parts were added, including the bell tower and the Church of Saint Catherine, which was rebuilt in 1880. The church's structure survives to this day, though the Muslims and the Turks looted and destroyed almost everything of value inside it, including ornaments, marble slabs, and even the lead roof. During the twentieth century the church was renovated and parts of it restored.

The Grotto of the Nativity is located beneath the church. The spot on which Jesus' birth took place is marked by a silver star on the eastern side of the cave. The star has fourteen points–the number of stations on the Via Dolorosa. The manger is in the Chapel of the Magi, on a lower level to the south. The Christmas Midnight Mass held at the Church of the Nativity is broadcast all around the world.

26-28 ◇ Shepherds' Field

The Franciscans identify the eastern end of the Arab village of Beit Sahur, near the field of Ruth the Moabite, as the Shepherds' Field. At the site is a grotto, over which a church commemorating the tidings of the angel to the shepherds has been built.

The Franciscan church, built in 1950, was designed by Italian architect Antonio Barluzzi. Its walls narrow as they approach the dome in a unique representation of a shepherd's tent. The glass apertures of the dome allow a great deal of light to penetrate the church, recalling the light that shone on the shepherds when the angel appeared (Luke 2:9). On the walls of the church are frescoes depicting the tidings to the shepherds and in the center is an altar resting on four bronze statues of shepherds.

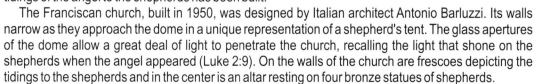

During excavations at the site, the remains of two monasteries were found–one from the fourth to the fifth centuries and another from the sixth century. An ancient watchtower that probably served to keep an eye on the flocks was also discovered, and its remains incorporated into the church building.

29-30 ◇ The Milk Grotto in Bethlehem

"When they had gone, an angel of the Lord appeared to Joseph in a dream. 'Get up,' he said, 'take the child and his mother and escape to Egypt. Stay there until I tell you, for Herod is going to search for the child to kill him'" (Matthew 2:13).

According to a very ancient tradition, Mary and the infant Jesus hid in this cave after the angel warned Joseph about Herod's intentions. As Mary was nursing the child, a drop of her milk fell on the rock, turning it white. Believers claim that the white stone of the cave has the power to increase the milk production of nursing mothers, and pilgrims often take fragments of the "Virgin's Milk" away with them. A Franciscan church has been built over the grotto.

32 ◇ The Road to Egypt

The road from Bethlehem to Egypt passes through the Judean Desert and the Sinai.

33 ◇ The Church of Saint Joseph in Nazareth

The tradition regarding the house of Joseph in Nazareth is based on medieval apocryphal literature. The Crusaders erected a church over the ruins of a Byzantine church at the site. In the mid-eighteenth century the Franciscans purchased the spot, which had lain in ruins for many years, and built a chapel dedicated to Joseph.

The present-day Church of Saint Joseph was built in 1914 on top of the remains of its predecessors. It has three naves that end along its eastern wall in three apses, and on the spot where the grotto, cistern, and baptismal font are located it is buttressed by man-made underground supports. In the crypt of the church are a cistern and mosaics, as well as grottos and granaries of ancient Nazareth.

34-36 ◇ The Baptismal Site on the Jordan near Jericho

The traditional baptismal site on the Jordan is about ten kilometers east of Jericho. In former times, when the spot accommodated many pilgrims, it was marked by a large wooden cross, at the place where it was said that "a voice came from heaven: 'You are my Son, whom I love; I am well pleased with you'" (Mark 1:11).

In the fourth century, the empress Helena gave orders to build two churches near the Jordan: one dedicated to John the Baptist and the other (constructed in the fifth century) to the prophet Elijah. Both churches were destroyed during the Muslim period, but during Crusader times the spot flourished anew. Close to the baptismal site stood the Monastery of John the Baptist, which was destroyed twice during the twelfth century—once by Muslims in 1140 and later in an earthquake—but rebuilt in 1169. When security conditions worsened during the Mameluke period, the monasteries on the Jordan were gradually abandoned. Conditions for pilgrimage became difficult, and pilgrims were exposed to harassment and hostility on the part of the local population. In the sixteenth century a new chapter in the baptismal tradition began, and has continued to the present day. As security conditions improved with the modern age, new churches, monasteries, and chapels were erected.

The earliest and most important of the monasteries on the Jordan was the Monastery of John the Baptist, which also commemorates the spot at which, according to tradition, the Israelites crossed the river. South of the baptismal site is a small octagonal chapel that was built in 1956 and is run by the Franciscans. Inside it is an altar surrounded by seats. Today, the baptism of pilgrims takes place at the conclusion of the pilgrimage to the holy places during Easter, and represents one of its high points.

37-38 ◇ The Quarantel Monastery

"Then Jesus was led by the Spirit into the desert to be tempted by the devil. After fasting for forty days and forty nights, he was hungry. The tempter came to him and said, 'If you are the Son of God, tell these stones to become bread.' Jesus answered, 'It is written: Man does not live by bread alone, but on every word that issues from the mouth of God'" (Matthew 4:1-4).

Near ancient Jericho is a mountain ridge that forms the western boundary of the Jordan Valley. Dotted with many caves, it is known as Mount Quarantel. Even though it served as an important center for nuns during the Byzantine period, the mountain was identified as the place where the devil tempted Jesus only later, in the Crusader period, at which time it also received the name Quarantel (from the Greek word for "forty," *quarantena*).

In 1874, the Greek Orthodox Patriarch began to build a monastery and a church on the mountain. He established the monastery at the midpoint of the slope over twenty-five hermit grottos. Today, the church dedicated to the Annunciation stands over one such cave, in which there once was a chapel. On the church's western wall is a collection of over one hundred icons, most of them from the eighteenth and nineteenth centuries. From the southeastern edge of the church, a flight of stairs leads to the Chapel of the Temptation, within which is the stone seat Jesus sat on while the devil tempted him. The stone is integrated into a niche with an altar above it.

39 ◇ The Pinnacle – The Highest Point of the Temple

"Then the devil led him to Jerusalem and had him stand on the highest point of the temple. 'If you are the Son of God,' he said, 'throw yourself down. For it is written: He will command his angels concerning you, and they will lift you up in their hands, so that you will not strike your foot against a stone.' Jesus answered him, 'It is also written: Do not put the Lord your God to the test'" (Matthew 4:5-7).

The highest point of the temple is identified with the southeastern corner of the Temple Mount, which rises high above its surroundings. Even after the Second Temple was destroyed, a great part of the retaining walls of the Temple Mount remained standing, and in the southeastern corner, which has been well preserved, stones from the time of Herod are visible in the wall.

40 ◇ The Mount of the Precipice

"He went to Nazareth, where he had been raised, and on the Sabbath day he went into the synagogue, as was his custom. And he stood up to read . . . All the people in the synagogue were furious when they heard this. They got up, drove him out of the town, and took him to the brow of the hill on which the town was built in order to cast him down the cliff. But he walked right through the crowd and went on his way" (Luke 4:16-30).

Already in ancient times, the mountain two-and-a-half kilometers southwest of Nazareth was identified as the Mount of the Precipice, from which the citizens of Nazareth wanted to throw Jesus down into the abyss. Its importance is demonstrated by the fact that in the ninth century, while in Nazareth there was only one church with twelve priests, eight priests served at the monastery on the Mount of the Precipice.

The Mount of the Precipice rises to a height of 230 meters above the Jezreel Valley, and appears from the valley to be a steep, soaring cliff. On its western side is a grotto. According to one tradition, the grotto opened up in order to provide Jesus (or Mary) with a hiding place at the crucial moment. A chapel dedicated to Mary was erected on the spot. Until 1970, the Franciscans held an annual mass on the Mount of the Precipice, but as a result of excavations that were carried out in the 1950s, in the course of which it became clear that ancient Nazareth was located on a hill to the north of the Basilica of the Annunciation, the tradition regarding the identity of the spot lost its importance.

41 ◇ Capernaum

Capernaum, on the shore of the Sea of Galilee, was the focal point of Jesus' activity in Galilee. He lived in the town, taught and gave sermons in its synagogue, and performed many miracles there, the most significant of which involved the resurrection of the daughter of Jairus. Despite the miracles, however, the residents of the town did not follow Jesus, for which he cursed Capernaum with destruction, along with nearby Korazin and Beit Saida.

Peter too lived in Capernaum: an octagonal church was built in the fifth century at the site identified with his house. Above the ruins of this ancient church, a new church, also octagonal in shape, has been constructed.

Capernaum was apparently founded in the second century BC. When Herod distributed his land among his sons, Capernaum became a border town and a customhouse was established there, intensifying the town's commercial activity. A church was built on the spot in the fourth century and a rise in the standard of living of the local inhabitants followed. There was a prosperous Jewish community in Capernaum during the entire Byzantine period until the end of the sixth century, when Jesus' prophecy was realized and Capernaum was destroyed in an earthquake. By the year 700, the city had ceased to exist.

In the photo are the remains of the town, the ruins of the synagogue, and the new church above the House of Peter.

42-43 ◇ Beit Saida Valley

The village of Beit Saida nestled in a valley on the eastern coast of the Sea of Galilee next to the mouth of the Jordan, near Capernaum. According to the story in John 1, the apostles Peter, Andrew, and Philip were fishermen from Beit Saida, which is also the place Jesus and his disciples went after they heard that Herod Antipas had killed John the Baptist.

Initially, Beit Saida was a poor fishing village. Philip, Herod's brother, elevated its status to that of a city, enlarged its area and population, and called it Julian in honor of the daughter of Emperor Augustus. The city was developed in two separate parts: the upper city, where Philip's palace and the public buildings stood, and the lower city, where the majority of the residents, most of whom were fisherman and farmers, resided.

44-45 ◇ Cana

"On the third day a wedding occurred in Cana in Galilee. Jesus' mother was there and Jesus and his disciples had also been invited to the wedding. When the wine was gone, Jesus' mother said to him, 'They have no more wine.' 'Dear woman, why do you involve me?' Jesus answered, 'My time has not yet come.' His mother said to the servants, 'Do whatever he tells you.' Nearby stood six stone water jars, the kind used by the Jews for ceremonial washing, each holding between twenty to thirty gallons. Jesus said to the servants, 'Fill the jars with water'; so they filled them to the brim. Then he told them, 'Now draw some out and take it to the master of the banquet.' They did so and the master of the banquet

tasted the water, which had been turned into wine. He did not realize where it had come from . . ." (John 2:1-9).

It was in Cana that Jesus began his ministry and performed his first miracle, turning water into wine. To commemorate the miracle, three churches were built in the village.

The Greek Orthodox church was erected in 1556 and rebuilt in 1886. Two stone jars, which the Greek Orthodox claim are two of the original six water jars, are kept in the church, which can be recognized from afar by its red domes.

The Franciscan church was built in 1879 over remains from the Byzantine and Crusader periods. The Crusaders had erected a large church divided by two rows of columns into a nave and two aisles on the spot. The current church is built mainly on the southern side of the Crusader church. To its north is a tiled courtyard from the fifth and sixth centuries and the remains of an earlier structure. A number of columns surviving from the Byzantine church are incorporated into the church's facade.

Before the altar stands a jar–a copy of one of the "original" jars that is now housed in Cologne, Germany. In the crypt are the remains of an ancient church, pieces of statues, coins, and four ancient columns. An ancient cistern and inscriptions that have also survived once belonged to a synagogue.The church has two towers, symbolizing the couple at the wedding, and a dome representing the family unit. In the north of the village is a Franciscan church dedicated to Saint Bartholomew (Nathanael), one of the twelve apostles, who was born in Cana. The church is built on the spot where, according to tradition, his house once stood.

46 ◇ The Lake of Gennesaret

"One day as Jesus was standing by the Lake of Gennesaret, with the people crowding around him and listening to the word of God, he saw two boats at the water's edge . . . He got into one of the boats, the one belonging to Simon, and asked him to put out a little from shore. Then he sat down and taught the people from the boat" (Luke 5:1-3).

The Lake of Gennesaret is one of the names for the Sea of Galilee. Ginnosar Valley lies on the northwestern side of the Sea of Galilee between Tabgha and Migdal, at the foot of Mount Arbel. In 1986, a boat from the time of Jesus was discovered in the Sea of Galilee in the area opposite Ginnosar Valley. The boat was removed from the water in its entirety and is on display at Kibbutz Ginnosar.

47 ◇ The Mount of Beatitudes

The Mount of Beatitudes above Tabgha is identified as the place where Jesus delivered the Sermon on the Mount to his disciples. The first church was built on the mountain's slope above a small cave. The new church, built on top of the hill in 1936, was designed by the Italian architect Antonio Barluzzi. From it, the Sea of Galilee, Capernaum, Tabgha, and other places connected with the early days of Jesus' ministry are visible.

48 ◇ Nain

"Soon afterward, Jesus went to a town called Nain, and his disciples and a large crowd went along with him. As he approached the town gates, a dead person was being carried out–the only son of his mother, and she was a widow. A large crowd from the town was with her. When the Lord saw her, his heart went out to her and he said, 'Don't cry.' Then he went up and touched the coffin, and those carrying it stood still. He said, 'Young man, I say to you, arise!' The dead man sat up and began to talk, and Jesus gave him back to his mother" (Luke 7:11-15).

Nain is located south of Mount Tabor, on the northern slope of Giv'at Hamore. According to tradition, it was here that Jesus revived the widow's son. In the Byzantine period there was a church on this spot but no detailed record of it exists. A hundred years ago it was possible to make out two ancient churches commemorating the events from Luke 7 here–one of them was near the village spring. As of yet, the dates regarding their construction and destruction are unknown.

In 1878 the place was acquired by the Franciscans, who built the current church in 1881. The modest church is decorated with two pictures dedicated to the miracle of the raising of the widow's son.

49 ◇ The Sea of Galilee during a Storm

"Then he got into the boat and his disciples followed him. Without warning, a furious storm blew up on the lake, so that the waves swept over the boat. But Jesus was sleeping. The disciples went and woke him, saying, 'Lord, save us! We're going to drown!' He replied, 'You of little faith, why are you so afraid?' Then he got up and rebuked the winds and the waves, and it was completely calm. The men were amazed and asked, 'What kind of man is this? Even the winds and the waves obey him!' (Matthew 8:23-27).

The Sea of Galilee is one of the holiest and most inspirational places in Christian tradition. Jesus lived here at the beginning of his ministry, and it was here that he found his first disciples. In the New Testament, the Sea of Galilee is also referred to as the Sea of Tiberias and the Lake of Gennesaret. At 212 meters below sea level, the Sea of Galilee is the lowest body of fresh water on earth. The source of most of its water is the Jordan River, which flows into it in the north and flows out of it in the south, making its way to the Dead Sea.

50-51 ◇ **Kursi**

"When he arrived at the other side in the region of the Gadarenes, two demon-possessed men coming from the tombs met him . . . 'What do you want with us, Son of God?' they shouted. 'Have you come here to torture us before the appointed time?' Some distance away, a large herd of pigs was feeding. The demons begged Jesus, 'If you drive us out, send us into the herd of pigs.' He said to them, 'Go!' So they came out and went into the pigs, and the whole herd rushed down the steep bank into the lake and drowned. Those tending the pigs ran off, went into the town and reported all this, including what had happened to the demon-possessed men. Then the whole town went out to meet Jesus. And when they saw him, they pleaded with him to leave their region" (Matthew 8:28-34).

The first Christians identified Kursi, on the eastern shore of the Sea of Galilee, as the site where the miracle of the swine took place, and a large monastery was built here in the fifth century. During the Persian invasion of 614, the monastery and its church were damaged and never regained their glory. The spot was destroyed by an earthquake at the beginning of the eighth century and the tradition of the church at Kursi is mentioned for the last time in the tenth century, after which the identification was forgotten.

In 1961, in the midst of road construction, the site's ancient remains were discovered. Extensive excavations were carried out, during which the monastery, church, and other sites around them were unearthed. It appears that the monastery at Kursi was the largest in the Holy Land during the fifth century. It was built according to a meticulous plan, with streets, a sewer system, public and residential buildings, as well as administrative, farm and fishing structures, and a hostel for pilgrims. The monastery's complex was enclosed by a wall, within which lived monks and members of the Christian community. Its main gate was on the west and a road led from it to the shore of the Sea of Galilee.

The church was designed as a symmetrical basilica, with two row of columns separating the nave from the two aisles. A small stone box of sacred relics was discovered at the site. The church was decorated with magnificent mosaics, many of which had flora and fauna motifs. Those depicting animals were apparently defaced by Muslims, and it may be that their treatment of the site is the reason there are no remains to connect Kursi with the miracle of the swine. On the mountain slope above Kursi's monastery, the sacred rock was discovered: it rises to a height of seven meters, marking the place Jesus met the demon-possessed man. Next to it are the remains of an ancient chapel.

52 ◇ **Capernaum from the Sea**

Capernaum, the city of Jesus, is one of the major attractions for pilgrims in the Holy Land and is mentioned in pilgrim literature from as early as the fourth century. It is possible to reach Capernaum in one of the many boats that traverse the Sea of Galilee, taking pilgrims to visit the holy sites along its shores.

53 ◇ **The Synagogue at Korazin**

"Then Jesus began to denounce the cities in which most of his miracles had been performed, because they did not repent. 'Woe to you, Korazin! Woe to you Beit Saida! If the miracles that were performed in you had been performed in Tyre and Sidon, they would have repented long ago in sackcloth and ashes. But I tell you it will be more bearable for Tyre and Sidon on the day of judgment than for you'" (Matthew 11:20-22).

Korazin reached the height of its fortune in the fourth century. In excavations carried out at the site, residential quarters, streets, an industrial zone, and a synagogue that probably dates back to the second or third century AD were discovered. The synagogue was built from black basalt stones characteristic of the region, and its design was similar to that of the ancient synagogue unearthed in Capernaum. It was richly adorned with stone decorations and geometric and floral reliefs. The facade of the synagogue, like that of the synagogue in Capernaum, faced Jerusalem. Three entrances led to a nave and two aisles with pews. Columns arranged in a horseshoe shape apparently supported a second floor. Among the findings was a stone chair with an Aramaic inscription probably used by the head of the synagogue.

54 ◇ **The Synagogue in Capernaum**

"Then he went down to Capernaum, a town in Galilee, and on the Sabbath began to teach the people. They were amazed at his teaching, because his message had authority. In the synagogue was a man . . ." (Luke 4:31-33).

The remains of Capernaum's synagogue were first discovered in 1838. The Franciscans purchased the site in 1894, and in 1921 the synagogue ruins were restored. Recently, after extensive excavations, researchers dated the synagogue to the fourth and fifth centuries.

The synagogue was built in the center of the settlement on the highest available spot, in accordance with Jewish law. Its design is similar to a basilica, with a nave, two aisles and an entrance via three openings from the south. At the entrance to the site, many fragments of the synagogue are scattered about. The decorations, carved in white limestone brought from afar, are evidence of the structure's magnificence. The synagogue was built over two layers of ancient foundations, but the synagogue mentioned in the New Testament, in which Jesus taught, inspiring awe with his sermons, has not yet been unearthed.

55 ◇ Jacob's Well

"So he came to a town in Samaria called Sychar, near the plot of ground Jacob had given his son Joseph. Jacob's well was there, and Jesus, tired as he was from the journey, sat down by the well. It was about the sixth hour. When a Samaritan woman came to draw water, Jesus said to her, 'Will you give me a drink?'" (John 4:5-7).

The identification of Jacob's Well is considered a certainty. The fact that it is the only well in the vicinity contributes to its claim to authenticity, as does its proximity to the main road, Joseph's Tomb, and Mount Gerizim. The first church was built over the well in the year 380, destroyed during the Samaritan rebellions of the fifth century, and rebuilt in the sixth century, during the days of Justinian.

The edges of the well were once adorned with a splendid mosaic (now at the Saint Sophia Church in Istanbul) depicting Jacob's Well surrounded by angels. During the Crusader period, the Church of Saint Savior was built on the spot. The Greek Orthodox purchased the site in 1860 and in 1914 began building a new church according to the design of the old Crusader church, but construction ceased after the Russian revolution due to lack of funds.

The edifice in which the well is located is the crypt of the Crusader church that was restored by the Greek Orthodox. In its eastern section is an altar, under which Jesus' stone seat can be found. The well, fifty meters deep, is located in front of the altar.

56-59 ◇ The Church of the Loaves and Fishes at Tabgha

"When Jesus landed and saw a large crowd, he had compassion on them and healed their sick. As evening approached, the disciples came to him and said, 'This is a remote place, and it's already getting late. Send the crowds away, so they can go to the villages and buy themselves some food.' Jesus replied, 'They do not need to leave. You give them something to eat.' 'We have only five loaves of bread and two fish,' they answered. 'Bring them here to me,' he said. And he directed the people to sit down on the grass. Taking the five loaves and the two fish and looking up to heaven, he gave thanks and broke the loaves. Then he gave them to the disciples, and the disciples gave them to the people. They all ate and were satisfied, and the disciples picked up twelve basketfuls of broken pieces that were left over. The number of those who ate was about five thousand men, besides women and children" (Matthew 14:14-21).

The valley known as Tabgha lies to the northwest of the Sea of Galilee, next to Capernaum. The name Tabgha, an Arabic corruption of the Greek word *heptapegon* ("seven springs") refers to the valley's seven ancient springs, which made the nearby shore one of the best fishing spots on the Sea of Galilee. The uninhabited valley was perfect for meetings of Jesus' followers, and it was here that the miracle of the loaves and fishes, the Sermon on the Mount, Jesus' appearance before his disciples after his death, and the transfer of primacy to Peter all occurred.

Tabgha was already known as the site where the miracle of the loaves and fishes occurred by the beginning of the Byzantine period. During excavations carried out at the site, remains of an ancient chapel from the year 350 and a Byzantine basilica with one of the most beautiful mosaics ever found in the Holy Land were unearthed. The basilica was designed in the shape of a cross, with one nave and two aisles separated by two rows of columns. The nave ends in a round apse with an altar above the stone on which, according to tradition, the miracle occurred. Nearby was discovered a mosaic depicting a pair of fish and a basket with loaves of bread. The church's courtyard was decorated with geometric mosaics, and along its edge were the monks' living quarters. The church was erected in the mid-fifth century and renovated at the end of the century, when the Greek inscriptions and the loaves and fish mosaic were added. Apparently, the church was destroyed at the beginning of the seventh century. The current church was built above its remains, and the nearby modern monastery was erected in 1956. Both belong to German Benedictine monks.

60 ◇ Susita

Susita was a Greek city about two kilometers east of the Sea of Galilee and 350 meters above it. The city, which existed from the Hellenistic period until the Arab conquest, was known by its Greek name Antiochia Hipos (*hipos* being the Greek word for "horse"). Pompey took it from the Jews and made it a free city of the Decapolis. Later, the emperor Augustus gave it to Herod, much to the displeasure of its inhabitants. After Herod's death the city passed to Syrian administration. The city limits reached the Sea of Galilee, and Susita was the rival of Jewish Tiberias across the lake. In the Byzantine period, many churches and public buildings were erected in the city, which was apparently destroyed around the time of the Arab invasion at the beginning of the seventh century.

61 ◇ Dalmanutha

Dalmanutha is mentioned in the New Testament once, when Jesus and his disciples set sail on the Sea of Galilee after he sends the people away following the second miracle of the loaves and fishes (Mark 8:10). Today the spot identified as Dalmanutha is marked by a large wooden cross placed on the Tabgha shore.

62 ◇ Caesarea Philippi

"When Jesus came to the region of Caesarea Philippi, he asked his disciples, 'Who do people say the Son of Man is?' They replied, 'Some say John the Baptist; others say Elijah; and still others, Jeremiah or one of the prophets.' 'But what about you?' he asked. 'Who do you say I am?' Simon Peter answered, 'You are the Christ, the Son of the living God'" (Matthew 16:13-16).

On the eve of his fateful trip to Jerusalem, Jesus journeyed as far as the foot of Mount Hermon, to the northern city of Caesarea Philippi, or Panias. The emperor Augustus gave the city of Panias to Herod, who gave it in turn to his son Philip, who enlarged it and called it Caesarea Philippi in order to distinguish it from other cities called Caesarea. According to the Evangelists, Jesus did not visit the city itself, but merely stayed nearby.

The Christian community arrived in Caesarea Philippi after fleeing Jerusalem before the Great Revolt. In the fourth century, the bishop of the city took part in the Nicaea conference, which indicates that it had an important Christian community. According to tradition, the bleeding woman whom Jesus healed on the outskirts of Capernaum was a resident of Caesarea Philippi. Eusebius records that before the doorway of her home stood a statue documenting the miracle of her healing. The statue was apparently destroyed in the fifth century by Emperor Julian, who switched it for a statue of himself, later struck by lightning. Christians collected the remains of the original statue and put them in a church that was apparently demolished during Muslim rule. The church's ruins were discovered in excavations carried out in recent years on the spot.

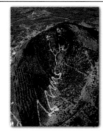

63-67 ◇ Mount Tabor

"After six days Jesus took with him Peter, James, and John the brother of James, and led them up a high mountain by themselves. There he was transfigured before them. His face shone like the sun, and his clothes became as white as the light. Just then there appeared before them Moses and Elijah talking with Jesus . . . While he was still speaking, a bright cloud enveloped them, and a voice from the cloud said, 'This is my Son, whom I love; I am well pleased with him. Listen to him!' When the disciples heard this, they fell to the ground, terrified. But Jesus came and touched them. 'Rise,' he said. 'Don't be afraid.' When they looked up, they saw no one except Jesus. As they were descending the mountain, Jesus instructed them, 'Don't tell anyone what you have seen, until the Son of Man has been raised from the dead'" (Matthew 17:1-9).

Mount Tabor has become sacred in Christian tradition as the Mount of the Transfiguration. In the Byzantine period, three churches and a monastery were established on the top of the mountain. When the Crusaders arrived at Mount Tabor they found a Greek Orthodox church on it, and they added a magnificent church and monastery to the site. The Sultan Baybars destroyed the churches on Mount Tabor in the thirteenth century, but believers continued to ascend the mountain in order to be among the ruins and to commemorate the Transfiguration, which is celebrated on August 6.

At the end of the nineteenth century the mountain was again settled by Franciscan monks, who built a monastery and a hostel on the summit. The current church, designed the architect Antonio Barluzzi, was constructed between 1919 and 1924. It is divided into a nave and two aisles, along the lines of the church from the Crusader period, and remains of the older structure were incorporated into the new. The two towers on the facade were built above two chapels from the Middle Ages, and are dedicated today to Moses and Elijah.

The excavated remains of the ancient monasteries and churches can be seen around the present-day church. The only element from the original basilica that has been positively identified is the mosaic floor outside the church's south wall.

On the northern part of the mountain stand the Church of Elijah and the Greek Orthodox monastery. The former was built over the remains of an earlier church from the Crusader period. West of the church, adjacent to its northwestern tower, is a cave commemorating the meeting of Abraham and Melchizedek.

68 ◇ Jericho

In the time of Jesus, Jericho was a magnificent city of majestic houses, a palace, public buildings, bathhouses, parks, and plazas. Like most of the Jews, Christians making pilgrimages to Jerusalem preferred to go by way of Jericho and not via Samaria, whose inhabitants, the Samaritans, were hostile. Jesus, on his way to Jerusalem for Passover, also passed through Jericho, where he restored a blind man's vision.

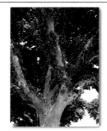

69 ◇ The Sycamore Tree

"Jesus entered Jericho and was passing through. A man by the name of Zacchaeus was there; he was a chief tax collector and was wealthy. He wanted to see who Jesus was, but being a short man, he could not, because of the crowd. So he ran ahead and climbed a sycamore-fig tree to see him, since Jesus was coming that way. When Jesus reached the spot, he looked up and said to him, 'Zacchaeus, come down immediately. I must stay at your house today.' So he came down at once and welcomed him gladly. All the people saw this and began to mutter, 'He has gone to be the guest of a sinner.' But Zacchaeus stood up and said to the Lord, 'Look, Lord! Here and now I donate half of my possessions to the poor, and if I have cheated anybody out of anything, I will pay back four times the amount.' Jesus said to him, 'Today salvation has come to this house, because this man, too, is a son of Abraham. For the Son of Man came to seek and to save what was lost'" (Luke 19:1-10).

The sycamore-fig tree that Zacchaeus climbed has been mentioned by pilgrims since the fourth century AD. To the present day, ancient sycamore trees identified with the sycamore-fig tree of Zacchaeus the tax collector can be seen in Jericho.

70-71 ◇ Bethany

Along the road leading from Jerusalem to Jericho, on the eastern slope of the Mount of Olives, lies the place usually identified as the village of Bethany (in Arabic, El-Azariya). During Jesus' final trip to Jerusalem, he stayed in Bethany at the house of Mary, Martha, and their brother Lazarus. Bethany was the point of departure for Jesus' victorious arrival in Jerusalem, and it was here that he raised Lazarus from the dead, one of his most important miracles.

Ancient Bethany lay to the west of the present-day village, as was discovered in excavations carried out at the site by the Franciscans. The expansion eastward, a process connected to the location of the reputed grave of Lazarus and the church built to the east of it, began in the Byzantine period.

72-73 ◇ The Eleona (The Church of the Pater Noster)

"Every day Jesus taught at the temple, and every evening he went out to spend the night on the hill called the Mount of Olives . . ." (Luke 21:37).

Tradition has it that the first church on this spot was built by the empress Helena, mother of the emperor Constantine, who erected a magnificent basilica on the place where Jesus liked to stay. The church was called "Eleon," Greek for "Mount of Olives." From the front of the church, which faces west, one could see Jerusalem–the same view seen by Jesus as he taught his disciples the principles of the faith.

The Byzantine church was destroyed during the Persian invasion. Using its remains, the Crusaders built a modest chapel on the spot, dubbing it Pater Noster after the prayer that begins "Our father who art in heaven." When the Crusader church made way for a more ornate church in 1152, the name Pater Noster persisted. The spot was razed later in the twelfth century by Saladin. In 1874, a monastery and church funded by the donation of an Italian princess were built on the site and given to the nuns of the Carmelite order.

On the walls of the cloister are tablets in dozens of languages with the verses of the Lord's Prayer.

74 ◇ The Pool of Siloam

"As he went along, he saw a man blind from birth . . . 'While I am in the world, I am the light of the world.' Having said this, he spat on the ground, made some mud with the saliva and put it on the man's eyes. 'Go,' he told him, 'wash in the Pool of Siloam' (this word means 'sent'). So the man went and washed and came home seeing" (John 9:1-7).

The Pool of Siloam is sacred to the Christians because Jesus miraculously healed a blind man there. In the fifth century, the empress Eudocia built a church dedicated to the miracle on the spot: its floor was in the Pool of Siloam itself. The church was constructed in an unusual direction, with its entrance from the north, apparently because of the difficulties of the site, and was divided into a nave and two aisles. The nave ended in a dome and an apse that were built over the opening of a tunnel. The pool became known for its healing powers, and was divided into two sections, one for women and the other for men. The church was destroyed in the Persian invasion of 614 and never restored. In order to prevent the rebuilding of the Christian site, the Muslims erected a mosque there. Today, a small pool is visible at one end of the tunnel.

75-77 ◇ The Tomb of Lazarus

"Take away the stone,' he said. 'But, Lord,' said Martha, the dead man's sister, 'by this time there is a bad odor, for he has been there four days.' Then Jesus said, 'Did I not tell you that if you believed, you would see the glory of God?' So they took away the stone. Then Jesus looked up and said, 'Father, I thank you that you have heard me. I knew that you always hear me but I said this for the benefit of the people standing here, that they may believe that you sent me.' When he had said this, Jesus called in a loud voice, 'Lazarus, come out!' The dead man came out, his hands and feet wrapped with strips of linen and a cloth around his face. Jesus said to them, 'Take off the grave clothes and let him go.' Therefore many of the Jews who had come to visit Mary, and had seen what Jesus did, put their faith in him" (John 11:39-45).

The raising of Lazarus not only caused great amazement among the crowd but also aroused the

anger of the Sanhedrin against Jesus, eventually bringing about the fateful decision to arrest and try him.

Bethany and the tomb of Lazarus are mentioned in pilgrim literature from as early as the beginning of the fourth century, at the end of which a church was built on the site of the grave. The first church was destroyed in an earthquake and rebuilt in the fifth and sixth centuries. Its main hall was on the east, its courtyard in the center, and the tomb of Lazarus to the west of the structure. The main ceremonies of Palm Sunday and Easter were held here on a mosaic floor with geometric patterns from this early period. In 1138, the church passed to the Benedictine monks of the Church of Saint Anne in Jerusalem, who erected a new church. This Crusader-period church, built on top of the former one, was dedicated to Martha and her sister Mary. Another church, built directly over the tomb of Lazarus, was dedicated to him and the miracle of his resurrection. After the expulsion of the Crusaders, both churches were destroyed, and from the fourteenth century on pilgrims testified that the Church of Lazarus had become a mosque. The current Franciscan church was built in 1954.

The tomb of Lazarus, which is located underneath the mosque, was carved in the soft limestone rock typical of the Mount of Olives. A corridor leads to a staircase down to the foyer. From there, a passageway leads to the room in which the tomb is located. The entrance was originally sealed with a stone, as it says in the Scriptures. The place where Jesus gave orders to roll the stone away from the grave has been made into a chapel. The altar on the site is in use today. Originally, there were three graves in the room, and according to tradition the one on the right is that of Lazarus. On the wall facing east, a passageway that connected the tomb with the Crusader church is visible, though it was blocked up by the Muslims when they built the mosque. In the sixteenth century the Franciscans carved out a new passage to the tomb that connects it with the street.

Nearby, on the road leading to Jericho, a Greek Orthodox church was also built. Opposite it is the round stone next to which, according to ancient tradition, Jesus and Martha met before Jesus raised Lazarus from the dead.

78-79 ◇ Bethphage

"As they approached Jerusalem and came to Bethphage on the Mount of Olives, Jesus sent two disciples, saying to them, 'Go to the village ahead of you, and at once you will find a donkey tied there with her colt by her. Untie them and bring them to me. If anyone says anything to you, tell him that the Lord needs them, and he will send them right away.' This took place to fulfill what was spoken through the prophet: 'Say to the Daughter of Zion, see, your king comes to you, gentle and riding on a donkey, on a colt, the foal of a donkey.' The disciples went and did as Jesus had told them. They brought the donkey and the colt, placed their cloaks on them, and Jesus sat on them. A very large crowd spread their cloaks on the road, while others cut branches from the trees and spread them on the road. The crowds that went ahead of him and those that followed shouted: 'Hosanna to the Son of David!' 'Blessed is he who comes in the name of the Lord!' 'Hosanna in the highest!' When Jesus entered Jerusalem, the whole city was stirred and asked, 'Who is it?' The crowds answered, 'It is Jesus, the prophet from Nazareth in Galilee'" (Matthew 21:1-11).

Bethphage is located on the southeastern part of the Mount of Olives, about one kilometer from Bethany. Christian tradition connects two events to this place: the conversation between Martha, Mary, and Jesus upon his return from beyond the Jordan to revive their brother Lazarus, and Jesus mounting the young donkey for his triumphant entrance into Jerusalem.

The church at Bethphage was built by Franciscans in 1883. In order not to attract the attention of the Muslim authorities, it was initially constructed as a regular house. The apse was added in 1897 and the bell tower only in 1954. The walls of the church are decorated with frescoes depicting Palm Sunday and Jesus' victorious entrance into Jerusalem. During excavations near the church, a stone decorated with paintings from the Crusader period was found. According to tradition, it is the stone from which Jesus mounted the young donkey. According to other traditions, the stone marks the meeting place of Jesus, Mary, and Martha.

Jesus' entrance into Jerusalem is commemorated in the Palm Sunday procession, which has set out from Bethphage since the Crusader period. The Muslim authorities forbade the procession in 1563, but it was renewed in 1933, and continues until today.

Pilgrimages are made to Bethphage on the Saturday before Palm Sunday.

80-81 ◇ Palm Sunday Mass

Palm Sunday begins with a mass in the Church of the Holy Sepulcher.

82-84 ◇ The Palm Sunday Procession Leaves Bethphage

At noon, the Palm Sunday procession leaves Bethphage in the direction of Jerusalem, via the Mount of Olives. The celebrants carry palm and olive branches while chanting "Hosanna, Hosanna."

85-87 ◇ The Church of Dominus Flevit on the Mount of Olives

"As he approached Jerusalem and saw the city, he wept over it and said, 'If you, even you, had only known on this day what would bring you peace—but now it is hidden from your eyes. The days will come upon you when your enemies will build an embankment against you and encircle you and hem you in on every side. They will dash you to the ground, you and the chidren within your walls. They will not leave one stone on another, because you did not recognize the time of God's coming to you'" (Luke 19:41-44).

Dominus flevit is Latin for "the Lord weeps." The cupola of the church is shaped like a teadrop, commemorating Jesus' weeping for Jerusalem. The church, designed by Antonio Barluzzi, was built by the Franciscans between 1954 and 1955 on the remains of a Byzantine church.

88-91◇ The Palm Sunday Procession

The procession descends the Mount of Olives, enters Jerusalem via the Lions' Gate, and ends in a ceremony in front of Saint Anne's Church next to the Bethesda Pool, also known as the Sheep's Pool.

92 ◇ The Hulda Steps at the Temple Mount

There were two gates in the southern wall of the Temple Mount—the western Hulda Gate, which was under the site of the present-day Al-Aqsa mosque, and the eastern Hulda Gate, which had three arched portals. The gates served as entrance and exit for visitors to the temple, and a monumental staircase, the remains of which were uncovered and restored in excavations carried out at the site, led to the western Hulda Gate. Jesus and his disciples ascended this staircase every time they entered the temple. Today, the two gates are blocked.

93 ◇ The Ruins of the Temple Mount

"As he was leaving the temple, one of his disciples said to him, 'Look, Teacher! What massive stones! What magnificent buildings!' 'Do you see all these grand buildings?' replied Jesus. 'Not one stone here will be left on another; every one will be thrown down'" (Mark 13:1-2).

The temple of the days of Jesus was the Second Temple, which was built in 536 BC on the remains of Solomon's Temple. In the days of Herod, it reached the height of its magnificence: people used to say that whoever had not seen the temple had never seen a magnificent building. The Second Temple was destroyed by the Romans in 70 AD.

94 ◇ The Mount of Olives

The Mount of Olives got its name from the olive groves that grew on it in ancient times. The mountain rises to a relatively great height, and commands a view of Jerusalem. Despite the fact that it is at a distance and somewhat isolated from the city, it is considered to be an inseparable part of it.

On the easternmost portion of the mountain lies Bethany, which Jesus often visited and where he performed the miracle of raising Lazarus. On the summit of the Mount of Olives is the grotto in which he taught his disciples the principles of the faith and from which he looked out on the city. In Gethsemane, at the foot of the slope, Jesus passed the night of agony before he was arrested. He traveled along the Mount of Olives when he entered Jerusalem riding on the young donkey, and was revealed to his disciples on the Mount of Olives after his death. It was also from here that he ascended to heaven.

The Mount of Olives is one of the most important holy sites for Christian pilgrims, and many churches have been built on it. Clerical life on the mountain has been lively since the fourth century. By the sixth century there were already twenty-four churches and monasteries on its slopes, among them the Church of Eleona, the Chapel of the Ascension, the church dedicated to Mary on the eastern portion of the mountain, a church dedicated to John the Baptist, and others. Today there are still many churches on the mountain, commemorating various events connected to the lives of Jesus and the Christian saints.

95 ◇ Mount Zion

Mount Zion is located in the southern part of Jerusalem's Old City. It rises to a height of seven hundred meters above sea level and borders Nahal Kidron. In ancient times, the mountain was within the walls of the city, but when the Turks rebuilt the city wall, most of the mountain remained outside of it.

On the top of Mount Zion are the Cenacle—the room of the Last Supper—the Tomb of David, and the Church of the Dormition, built on the spot where Jesus' mother Mary fell asleep. On the slope of the mountain are the Church of Saint Peter in Gallicantu and the Armenian Church of Caiaphas.

96 ◇ The Cenacle on Mount Zion

"On the first day of the Feast of Unleavened Bread, when it was customary to sacrifice the Passover lamb, Jesus' disciples asked him, 'Where do you want us to go and make preparations for you to eat the Passover?' So he sent two of his disciples, saying to them, 'Go into the city, and a man carrying a jar of water will meet you. Follow him. Say to the owner of the house he enters, 'The Teacher asks: Where is my guest room, where may I eat the Passover with my disciples?' He will show you a large upper room, furnished and ready. Make preparations for us there.' The disciples left, went into the city and found things just as Jesus had told them. So they prepared the Passover. When evening came, Jesus arrived with the Twelve. While they were reclining at the table eating, he said, 'I tell you truly, one of you will betray me—one who is eating with me.' They were saddened and one by one said to him, 'Surely not I?' 'It is one of the Twelve,' he replied, 'one who dips bread into the bowl with me. The Son of Man will go just as it is written about him. But woe to that man who betrays the Son of Man! It would be better for him if he had not been born.' While they were eating, Jesus took bread, gave thanks and broke it, and gave it to his disciples, saying, 'Take it; this is my body.' Then he took the cup, gave thanks and offered it to them, and they all drank from it. 'This is my blood of the covenant, which is poured out for many,' he said to them. 'I tell you the truth, I will not drink again of the fruit of the vine until that day when I drink it anew in the kingdom of God'" (Mark 14:12-25).

According to tradition, the "large upper room" where the Last Supper took place was on the Mount of Olives. The room of the Last Supper is called the *coenaculum* ("dining room" in Latin). After the crucifixion, the disciples gathered in this room together with other believers, including Mary, Jesus' mother. It was here that Jesus appeared before his disciples after rising from the dead, that the Holy Spirit descended on the disciples at Pentecost, and that the first core of Christian believers was formed.

In the year 390, a large basilica called Hagia Zion was erected on Mount Zion, and a small chapel dedicated to the Last Supper built in its northeastern corner. The church was considered the Mother of the Churches of Zion, and was one of the earliest, largest, and most important churches in Jerusalem.

The Byzantine church was destroyed in 996. In its stead, the Crusaders built a large, ornate church with a special chapel dedicated to the Dormition. This church was destroyed in 1219, and of it only two small chapels remain: the Dormition and the Cenacle, which includes the Tomb of David. The Franciscans purchased the place in 1335 and restored the Cenacle. In the first half of the fifteenth century, it passed into the hands of Muslims, who transformed it into a mosque and installed a mihrab—a niche indicating the direction of Mecca, to which Muslims turn in prayer. In 1948, members of all faiths received the right to pray there.

In the course of renovations carried out in 1960, the remains of a wall and decorations from the Crusader period were found.

97-101 ◇ The Ritual Foot-Washing on Holy Thursday

"[S]o he got up from the meal, took off his outer clothing, and wrapped a towel around his waist. After that, he poured water into a basin and began to wash his disciples' feet, drying them with the towel that was wrapped around him. He came to Simon Peter, who said to him, 'Lord, are you going to wash my feet?' Jesus replied, 'You do not realize what I am doing, but later you will understand.' 'No,' said Peter, 'you shall never wash my feet.' Jesus answered, 'Unless I wash you, you have no part with me'" (John 13:4-8).

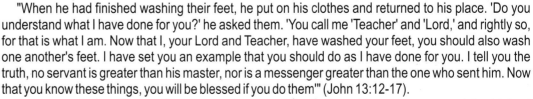

"When he had finished washing their feet, he put on his clothes and returned to his place. 'Do you understand what I have done for you?' he asked them. 'You call me 'Teacher' and 'Lord,' and rightly so, for that is what I am. Now that I, your Lord and Teacher, have washed your feet, you should also wash one another's feet. I have set you an example that you should do as I have done for you. I tell you the truth, no servant is greater than his master, nor is a messenger greater than the one who sent him. Now that you know these things, you will be blessed if you do them'" (John 13:12-17).

Every year before Easter, Christian sects reenact the foot-washing ceremony, and the highest prelate of each church washes the feet of a dozen members of the lower clergy. The date of the Roman Catholic ceremony is determined according to the Gregorian calendar, while the ceremonies of the Eastern churches follow the Julian calendar.

The Armenian Catholic ceremony, during which the feet of twelve children are washed by the archbishop, is held in the Polish church, which is currently in the Armenians' possession. During the Roman Catholic ceremony, the Latin Patriarch washes the feet of six novices. At the end of the ceremony, each of them receives a small silver crucifix.

The Ethiopian ceremony takes place at the Deir el-Sultan (the Ethiopian courtyard situated on the roof of Saint Helena's Chapel in the Church of the Holy Sepulcher). The ceremony is held inside a large tent erected especially for the Passover. After the archbishop and the twelve candidates have made

seven circuits inside the tent, the archbishop takes off his splendid mantle and crown, dons a white gown, and rubs the feet of the twelve with water and grape leaves.

The Greek Orthodox ceremony is the most impressive of the various foot-washing ceremonies, and is conducted on a podium erected for this purpose in the courtyard before the entrance of the Church of the Holy Sepulcher (the atrium). During the ceremony, the courtyard and surrounding balconies and roofs are packed with a dense throng of believers. On each side of the podium are seated half a dozen members of the lower clergy, with the Patriarch in the middle. Two assistants divest the Patriarch of his ceremonial robe and his resplendent crown, then wrap him in a white gown. The Patriarch bends down and washes, and afterwards wipes, a foot of each of those sitting before him. When all of them have had their feet washed, the Patriarch rinses his hands in clean water, dons his ceremonial robes once again, and returns to the patriarchate. Along the route, he dips a bouquet of flowers in the water that has been used for the foot-washing and sprinkles it on the faithful.

102 ◇ The Stairs to the Kidron Valley

An ancient staircase leads from Mount Zion to the Kidron Valley. According to tradition, Jesus descended it after the Last Supper, and later ascended it with his captors to the house of the high priest Caiaphas.

103 ◇ The Olive Grove in Gethsemane

"When he had finished praying, Jesus left with his disciples and crossed the Kidron Valley. On the other side was an olive grove, and he and his disciples entered it" (John 18:1).

"They went to a place called Gethsemane, and Jesus said to his disciples, 'Sit here while I pray'" (Mark 14:32).

In ancient times, Gethsemane was agricultural in character, with an olive grove and an olive press. It is clear that it was situated outside of Jerusalem's wall, since according to the law at the time, fruit trees and groves had to be at a distance of at least twenty-five feet from the city wall. Because of the foul stench of fertilizer, it was strictly forbidden to plant gardens inside the city. The olive trees in Gethsemane are very old. Josephus Flavius testifies that during the siege on Jerusalem, the Romans destroyed the trees in the vicinity of the city, but since olive trees can grow new branches even after they are cut down, it is possible that these are the same trees beneath which Jesus sat.

104-105 ◇ The Grotto at Gethsemane

"Now Judas, who betrayed him, knew the place, because Jesus had often met there with his disciples" (John 18:2).

Jesus and his disciples went to the grotto at Gethsemane frequently to hide and pray. According to tradition, this is the place for which Jesus and his disciples set out after partaking of the Passover meal and reading a hymn on the Mount of Olives. Jesus parted from his disciples at Gethsemane, and it was to Gethsemane that Judas Iscariot returned with the crowd to give Jesus the kiss of betrayal. In the fourth century the grotto became a chapel commemorating the disciples' prayer and Jesus' arrest. It was renovated in 1956, and three altars installed: the central one dedicated to Jesus' prayer among the disciples, the left-hand one to the ascension of Mary, and the right-hand one to Judas' kiss of betrayal.

106-110 ◇ The Church of All Nations (Basilica of the Agony) in Gethsemane

"He withdrew about a stone's throw beyond them, knelt down and prayed, 'Father, if you are willing, take this cup from me; yet not my will, but yours be done.' An angel from heaven appeared to him and strengthened him. And being in anguish, he prayed more earnestly, and his sweat was like drops of blood falling to the ground. When he rose from prayer and went back to the disciples, he found them asleep, exhausted from sorrow. 'Why are you sleeping?' he asked them. 'Get up and pray so that you will not fall into temptation'" (Luke 22:41-46).

The Church of All Nations at Gethsemane is also called the Basilica of the Agony, and it symbolizes the place where Jesus was "overwhelmed with sorrow to the point of death." The church at Gethsemane is first mentioned in the fourth century by the pilgrim Egeria, who tells of a religious procession from the Church of the Ascension to Gethsemane. The first church, which had impressive pillars with Corinthian capitals, was built on a steep slope. It was destroyed in the Persian invasion and rebuilt by the Crusaders, who called it the Church of Saint Savior.

The present-day church, built by the Franciscan architect Antonio Barluzzi, was inaugurated in 1924. In order to effect an atmosphere of anguish, the ceiling of the church was lowered by means of twelve domes strewn with stars on a blue background, olive branches adorning the corners. In addition, the light in the church was made softer by means of semi-opaque windows, and a portion of the original rock was left in its original form.

The church was built over the Rock of Agony, according to tradition the rock next to which Jesus prayed to God that the "cup be taken from me." The rock is surrounded by a balustrade of iron cast as a crown of thorns. On the front is a pair of birds next to a cup, and on either side, a pair of doves stretch out their necks for martyrdom.

Many nations took part in the building of the church (hence its name), and their symbols decorate its apses and domes. The church is one of the most beautiful in Jerusalem, and is second in religious importance only to the Church of the Holy Sepulcher.

111 ◇ Judas' Kiss

"Just as he was speaking, Judas, one of the Twelve, appeared. With him was a crowd armed with swords and clubs, sent from the chief priests, the teachers of the law, and the elders. Now the betrayer had arranged a signal with them: 'The man I kiss is the man; arrest him and take him away under guard.' Going at once to Jesus, Judas said, 'Rabbi!' and kissed him" (Mark 14:43-45).

"[B]ut Jesus asked him, 'Judas, are you betraying the Son of Man with a kiss?'" (Luke 22:48).

The kissing scene is depicted in a mosaic in the Basilica of the Agony. The spot on which the kiss took place is marked by a column within a niche in the rock opposite the apse of the Basilica of the Agony on the side of the road ascending from Gethsemane to the Mount of Olives.

112-113 ◇ The Church of Saint Peter in Gallicantu (The House of Caiaphas)

"Then seizing him, they led him away, taking him to the house of the high priest. Peter followed at a distance. But when they had kindled a fire in the middle of the courtyard and sat down together, Peter sat down with them. A servant girl saw him seated there in the firelight. She looked closely at him and said, 'This man was with him.' But he denied it. 'Woman, I don't know him,' he said. A little later someone else saw him and said, 'You also are one of them.' 'Man, I am not!' Peter replied. About an hour later another asserted, 'Certainly this fellow was with him, for he is a Galilean.' Peter replied, 'Man, I don't know what you're talking about!' Just as he was speaking, the rooster crowed. The Lord turned and looked straight at Peter. Then Peter remembered the word the Lord had spoken to him: 'Before the rooster crows today, you will disown me three times.' And he went outside and wept bitterly" (Luke 22:54-62).

This church is dedicated to Peter, who thrice denied the Lord when he was being interrogated at the house of the high priest Caiaphas. The name Gallicantu ("the cry of the rooster" in Latin) relates to Peter's successive denials just before the crow of the rooster, as Jesus had prophesied after the Passover meal.

In 457, Empress Eudocia built a church over the remains of Caiaphas' house in order to commemorate both the denial and the contrition. The church was apparently destroyed in 614, at the time of the Persian invasion, but was mentioned again in historical records a short while afterwards. In the tenth century, the church was again demolished, and later rebuilt by the Crusaders. By the beginning of the twelfth century it had acquired the name "Gallicantu." The Crusader church was destroyed in 1330.

The current church, inaugurated in 1931, was constructed in levels on the slope of the mountain, and is conspicuous from a distance, as it is built in an open place on the eastern slope of Mount Zion descending steeply in the direction of the village of Siloam and the Kidron Valley. Inside the church, a staircase leads to underground rooms. An additional level, identified as guardrooms, once housed prison cells, and hooks for chains are visible. According to tradition, the apostles were imprisoned and beaten in these rooms, which they left after their liberation to teach at the temple. A lower level has crosses carved in stone, possibly the work of Byzantine pilgrims.

113 ◇ The Ossuary of the High Priest Caiaphas

The ossuary of the high priest Caiaphas was discovered in a burial grotto in Jerusalem and is on display in the Israel Museum in Jerusalem.

114 ◇ The Prison of Christ

Next to the Convent of the Sisters of Zion, the Greek Orthodox have identified the Prison of Christ–the place where Jesus was held before his trial. In 1906, the Greek Orthodox established a church on the spot. The church has rooms and niches carved in the rock. In one of them–the place of incarceration identified as the Prison of Christ–is a sort of rack. One room is identified as the place where Barabbas was imprisoned.

115 ◇ The Antonia Fortress

The Antonia Fortress was built by Herod in the year 10 BC on the ruins of an ancient fortress. It was named after Mark Anthony, who had crowned Herod king of Judea.

The Antonia, which perches on an escarpment of natural rock, overlooked the Temple Mount and served as a base for the Roman garrison in Jerusalem, the seat of the Roman governor, and a courthouse–the Praetorium. In the days of the Second Temple, the troops in the fortress were reinforced during holidays in order to ensure that rebellion would not break out among the masses of pilgrims who were lodging in the capital. That fear may explain the presence in Jerusalem of Pontius

Pilate, the Roman governor, whose usual place of residence was Caesarea. Today, the Muslim Omariye College is located in the Antonia compound.

116 ◇ The Church of the Flagellation

According to tradition, this is the place where Jesus was flagellated by Roman soldiers after his sentence was handed down (Matthew 27:27-30).

A church was first built here in the Middle Ages, apparently, but underwent many transformations: after serving as a stable and a weaver's store, it was finally completely demolished. In 1838, Ibrahim Pasha gave the place to the Franciscans, who restored it. The church was rebuilt in 1927, and today its most impressive elements are the three windows depicting Barabbas' cries of triumph upon being released, the flagellation of Jesus (seen adorned with a crown of thorns among Roman soldiers), and Pilate washing his hands of culpability.

117 ◇ The Ecce Homo Arch

The Ecce Homo Arch is part of a Roman triumphal gate with three portals. The northern, lower arch is integrated into the Ecce Homo Chapel, in whose basement is the Convent of the Sisters of Zion. According to tradition, it was under this arch that Pilate presented Jesus to the Jews with the words "Here is the Man!" ("Ecce Homo"). Because of its connection to that tradition, the arch was also called "Pilate's Arch."

118-119 ◇ The Lithostrotos

Jesus' trial before Roman governor Pontius Pilate was conducted at the Praetorium, at a place know as the Stone Pavement, in Latin, *lithostrotos*. Pilate sat "on the judge's seat." The flagstones identified with the Lithostrotos begin to the north of the Tower of Antonia and continue up to the Convent of the Sisters of Zion.

120 ◇ Pontius Pilate

Pontius Pilate was the Roman governor in the days of Jesus, and it was Pilate who judged him and sentenced him to crucifixion. Pilate's permanent place of residence was Caesarea, and the theory is that he was in Jerusalem out of fear that a rebellion would break out at Passover, when throngs of pilgrims were concentrated in the city. Pontius Pilate's name appeared carved on a stone found in excavations carried out in Caesarea.

121 ◇ Via Dolorosa - The Way of the Cross

"And when they had mocked him, they took off the purple robe and put his own clothes on him. Then they led him out to crucify him. A certain man from Cyrene, Simon, the father of Alexander and Rufus, was passing by on his way in from the country, and they forced him to carry the cross. They brought Jesus to the place called Golgotha (which means 'The Place of the Skull'). Then they offered him wine mixed with myrrh, but he did not take it. And they crucified him. Dividing up his clothes, they cast lots to see what each would receive. It was the third hour when they crucified him. The written notice of the charge against him read: THE KING OF THE JEWS" (Mark 15:20-26).

The Via Dolorosa leads from the Praetorium to the Church of the Holy Sepulcher. During the week it is a street like all others, but once a week, on Friday afternoon, the Procession of the Cross travels the entire length of the Way of the Sorrow.

Of the fourteen stations that comprise the Via Dolorosa, nine are along the way to the Church of the Holy Sepulcher and five are inside it. Eight of the outside stations are commemorated by churches or small chapels, and additional chapels and holy sites connected with Jesus' final path dot the route.

122 ◇ Station I: Jesus Is Condemned to Death

"Then the Jews led Jesus from Caiaphas to the palace of the Roman governor. By now it was early morning, and to avoid ceremonial impurity the Jews did not enter the palace" (John 18:28).

"When Pilate heard this, he brought Jesus out and sat down on the judge's seat at a place known as the Stone Pavement (which in Aramaic is 'Gabbatha'). It was the day of Preparation of Passover Week, about the sixth hour. 'Here is your king,' Pilate said to the Jews. But they shouted, 'Take him away! Take him away! Crucify him!' 'Shall I crucify your king?' Pilate asked. 'We have no king but Caesar,' the chief priests answered. Finally Pilate handed him over to them to be crucified" (John 19:13-16).

Station I is located in the courtyard of Omariye College. The current building was built in the Mameluke period on the foundations of the Antonia Fortress from the time of Herod. There is no church or chapel on the spot to commemorate the incident from John 19, but during the Crusader period a chapel commemorating the crowning of Jesus with thorns was erected in the southern portion of the courtyard, only to be destroyed by an earthquake in 1927. (See also 115.)

123 ◇ Station II: Jesus Takes Up the Cross

"Then the governor's soldiers took Jesus into the Praetorium and gathered the whole company of soldiers round him. They stripped him and put a scarlet robe on him, and then twisted together a crown of thorns and set it on his head. They put a staff in his right hand and knelt in front of him and mocked him. 'Hail, king of the Jews!' they said. They spat on him, and took the staff and struck him on the head again and again. After they had mocked him, they took off the robe and put his own clothes on him. Then they led him away to crucify him" (Matthew 27:27-31).

Station II is in the Chapel of the Condemnation, next to the Church of the Flagellation. The chapel, which was renovated by the Franciscans in 1903, was built over the remains of a Byzantine church and is similar to it in form. On the western side of its floor are large grooved stones–part of the Lithostrotos. Outside the chapel is a stone marking the beginning of the Lithostrotos.

124-125 ◇ Station III: Jesus Falls for the First Time

For many years, Station III was marked by two broken columns. In 1947, a new chapel was built on the spot with the help of donations from Polish soldiers who were in the Holy Land at the time. Today, a museum with an archaeological collection is located at the site.

126 ◇ Station IV: Jesus is Met by His Mother

Station IV is located in a chapel marked by a lintel depicting Jesus and his mother. A few steps away is the Armenian Catholic church, built in 1881 and dedicated to Mary. In a crypt constructed on the level of the ancient road is a mosaic floor that was uncovered during the building of the church and integrated into its design: at its center is the image of a pair of sandals. The floor may belong to a church from the fifth and sixth centuries. The sandals were mentioned in texts from the fourteenth century as marking the place where Mary stood while her son passed by carrying the cross.

126-127 ◇ Station V: Simon the Cyrene Helps Jesus Carry the Cross

"As they led him away, they seized Simon from Cyrene, who was on his way in from the country, and put the cross on him and made him carry it behind Jesus" (Luke 23:26).

Station V, dedicated to Simon the Cyrene, is located at the corner of the street. The current chapel was built by the Franciscans in 1895. Until then, the spot was marked by a grooved stone mounted on the wall.

128 ◇ Station VI: Veronica Wipes Jesus' Face

Station VI is marked by a column recessed in the wall. According to tradition, this was the home of Veronica, who approached Jesus with a damp handkerchief and wiped the sweat from his face. Tradition has it that the image of Jesus' face was imprinted on the handkerchief. Another legend says that Veronica was invited to Rome by Emperor Tiberius, who was cured of an illness after gazing at the cloth. Today, a handkerchief believed to be Veronica's is kept in Saint Peter's in Rome.

The spot was purchased by the Greek Catholics in 1883, and two years later the Church of Saint Veronica was built there, apparently on top of the remains of a sixth-century church.

129 ◇ Station VII: Jesus Falls for the Second Time

This station is known as the Judgement Gate. Legend has it that the city gate upon whose threshold Jesus fell under the burden of the cross was located here. Inside the chapel, which belongs to the Copts, is a tall column that has survived from the double row of columns that once lined the length of the Cardo Maximus–the main street of the Roman city.

130 ◇ Station VIII: Jesus Speaks to the Women of Jerusalem

This station is situated outside of the Second Temple period city limits, so that the meeting with the women of Jerusalem who wept over the bitter fate of Jesus must have occurred in the open field. The station is marked by a stone bearing a cross and a Latin inscription with the message "Jesus Christ is Victorious" mounted on the wall. The place is near Golgotha, but access is blocked by a Greek Orthodox church.

131 ◇ Station IX: Jesus Falls for the Third Time

Further along the road in the direction of the Church of the Holy Sepulcher is a staircase on the right ascending to Deir el-Sultan, which perches on the roof of the Church of the Holy Sepulcher. A column that has survived from the Roman Cardo marks Station IX, where Jesus fell for the third time.

132 ◇ The Church of the Holy Sepulcher

The Church of the Holy Sepulcher was established by Emperor Constantine in the fourth century. The emperor gave orders to erect a church that would surpass all others in its beauty, and construction took from 326 to 335. The result was the largest church in the entire Byzantine world, and people came from all over the empire to be present at its consecration. The church complex included several buildings, the most important of which were the rotunda built over the tomb and crowned with a dome, the basilica, and the courtyard situated between them.

Next to the courtyard to the southeast was Golgotha. During the construction of the Byzantine church, the edges of Golgotha were carved away and it was given the form of a large cube rising to a height of about five meters. At the foot of Golgotha, pilgrims were shown the place of the binding of Isaac and the meeting between Abraham and Melchizedek, also believed to be the center of the world. On Golgotha's summit, clerical leaders were ordained and during Easter the chapters relating to the suffering of Jesus were read. Golgotha was first incorporated within the church's precincts during the Crusader period, at which time it was also decorated with splendid mosaics.

When the Persians conquered Jerusalem in 614, the Church of the Holy Sepulcher was torched and the True Cross taken. In 628, Emperor Heraclius defeated the Persians and the cross was returned in triumph to Jerusalem.

When the Muslims conquered Jerusalem, the Christians lost control of the Church of the Holy Sepulcher. In 935, the Muslims confiscated the southwestern part of the courtyard and built a small mosque there. In 1009 the Egyptian caliph Al-Hakim gave orders to raze the church to the ground, leaving only the foundations of the rotunda. The church was restored by Emperor Constantine Monomachus in 1018.

When the Crusaders conquered Jerusalem, the church returned for a time to Christian proprietorship. In 1187 Jerusalem fell into the hands of Saladin, and the keys to the church were turned over to the Muslims, though for a fee the Christians retained the right to both pray at and maintain the holy places there. The church's present-day appearance is preserved mainly from the Crusader period. The Crusader church complex, which was consecrated in 1149, included all of the proximate holy sites in one edifice. The Chapel of Golgotha, besides being heightened, was included in the church for the first time.

The Crusaders built a large dome decorated with mosaics over the rotunda. It was restored by the Franciscans, at beginning of the eighteenth century at which time the remains of the Crusader mosaics were removed. In 1808, a fire broke out in the Church of the Holy Sepulcher–the dome of the rotunda collapsed, the columns cracked, and the stability of the building was undermined. This time the rotunda was restored by the Greek Orthodox. The appearance of the rotunda was greatly altered in the course of the renovations, though in recent years great effort has been expended to restore it to its original form.

On the site of Constantine's basilica, east of the rotunda, the Crusaders built a large church that has survived almost in its entirety. Its dome is the largest of its kind in Israel. Today, the church hall–the Catholicon (Greek for "general")–is in Greek Orthodox hands, and serves as their central prayer hall in the Church of the Holy Sepulcher. After the 1808 fire, the hall was walled up. In the center of the Catholicon is a stone chalice marking the navel of the world.

Northwest of the rotunda is the chapel commemorating Jesus' appearance before his mother after his resurrection. Today it serves as the central church of the Franciscans in the Church of the Holy Sepulcher. To the right of its altar is the Pillar of the Flagellation, to which Jesus was bound by the Roman soldiers during his trial at the Praetorium. A fragment of the True Cross was on display on the central altar until the sixteenth century, when the holy relic was stolen.

133 ◇ The Atrium of the Church of the Holy Sepulcher

The atrium of the Church of the Holy Sepulcher has not changed much since the twelfth century. To its south rises the Mosque of Omar, commemorating the prayer of the caliph Omar on the steps of the church after the Muslim conquest. Nearby is a Greek Orthodox monastery built over the remains of a monastery from the Crusader period.

On the south the atrium is bordered by a portico. On the west it is lined by chapels, most of which belong to the convent of the Greek Orthodox Patriarchate. On its north is the Armenian chapel, above which towers the belfry, and to its east is the Greek Orthodox monastery dedicated to the patriarch Abraham. In the upper part of the monastery, a special area has been set aside for Anglican worship. North of it are the Armenian Chapel of Saint John and the Coptic Chapel of Saint Michael, from which a staircase leads to the Ethiopian chapel and the Deir el-Sultan Monastery on the roof of the church.

134-137 ◇ The Entrance to the Church of the Holy Sepulcher

The facade of the church is numbered among the loveliest Crusader remains in the Holy Land. In times past, the gates were decorated with colorful mosaics and rich stonework (the Crusader lintel decorations, which were removed, are on display today at the Rockefeller Museum). The eastern gate was apparently blocked up in the twelfth century on orders of Saladin, and it remains so today.

The staircase on the right once led to a portico that was later transformed into a chapel dedicated to Mary: it serves as Station X on the Via Dolorosa. During the Crusader period, it was an open, decorated portico that enabled direct access to Golgotha. The portal to Golgotha was also blocked up at the end of the twelfth century, at which time the gate leading to it became a window.

West of the facade, a Crusader belfry rises to a height of five stories. After Saladin's conquest of Jerusalem, the bells in the tower were destroyed and it was not used again until the end of the nineteenth century. The upper story of the tower collapsed in the sixteenth century, and at the beginning of the eighteenth century two-and-a-half additional stories were leveled for fear they would collapse on the dome.

138 ◇ Christ's Prison Chapel

This is a small low windowless room carved out of the rock and reached via a set of steps. According to tradition, Jesus was held here until his crucifixion. Under the altar in the chapel is a stone with two round openings, to which, according to tradition, Jesus' legs were chained.

139 ◇ Station X: Jesus is Stripped of His Garments

This station is in the Chapel of the Sorrows, though the portal to the chapel is closed and you can only see into it from the window at Station XI. During the Crusader period, this room served as the entrance to Golgotha. The room, along with its unusual dome and rich decorations, has been preserved in its entirety. With the Muslim conquest of 1187, the entrance to Golgotha was blocked up, and in its place, a window installed. Today the chapel is in the hands of the Latin Patriarchate and is dedicated to Jesus' mother Mary and John the Baptist.

140 ◇ Station XI: Jesus is Nailed to the Cross

Station XI, XII, and XIII are on Golgotha, where Jesus' suffering came to an end. Golgotha is divided into two main chapels: the right-hand one belongs to the Latin Patriarchate (Station XI), the one on the left belongs to the Greek Orthodox (Station XII), and between them is Station XIII, which is under Franciscan control. Golgotha is the navel of the world, the site of the binding of Isaac, and the locus of the crucifixion. Here Adam was created from dust and here his skull is buried.

The silver altar in Station XI is from the period of the Renaissance, and was donated to the church by the Duke de Medici from Tuscany in 1588. On the wall above it is a mosaic depicting Jesus nailed to the cross. Above him stand Mary and John, and on the ceiling, a Crusader mosaic depicts him ascending to heaven.

141-143 ◇ Station XII: Jesus Dies on the Cross

Below the altar in this chapel, currently under Greek Orthodox control, hangs a silver disk, in the middle of which is a hole signifying where the cross was placed. Two additional black disks on either side of the altar mark the crucifixion sites of the two thieves. To the right of the altar, under a metal cover, the crevice created in the rock when the cross was fixed in it is visible. The fissure reaches the Chapel of Adam below.

144 ◇ Station XIII: Jesus is Taken Down from the Cross

This station is located between Station XI and Station XII. Here Mary took Jesus' body in her arms after he was taken down from the cross. The altar at the station, called the Altar of Our Lady of Sorrows (Mater Dolorosa), is dedicated to Mary. On it is a sixteenth-century gold-plated statue of the Madonna, with precious stones and a gold crown. The statue was brought to the church from Lisbon in 1788, and is kept in a glass cabinet, around which hang gold gifts offered by pilgrims.

145 ◇ The Place of the Three Women
In the church's vestibule, near the Stone of the Anointing, is the place where Jesus' mother Mary stood with other women during the crucifixion. The place is currently in the hands of the Armenians.

146-147 ◇ The Stone of the Anointing in the Church of the Holy Sepulcher
"Later, Joseph of Arimathea asked Pilate for the body of Jesus. Now Joseph was a disciple of Jesus, but secretly, because he feared the Jews. With Pilate's permission, he came and took the body away. He was accompanied by Nicodemus, the man who earlier had visited Jesus at night. Nicodemus brought a mixture of myrrh and aloes, about seventy-five pounds. Taking Jesus' body, the two of them wrapped it with the spices in strips of linen, in accordance with Jewish burial custom" (John 19:38-40).

The Stone of the Anointing is located just inside the entrance to the Church of the Holy Sepulcher. Three pairs of candelabra flank the stone, representing the Franciscans, the Greek Orthodox, and the Armenians.

According to tradition, after Jesus was brought down off the cross, Joseph of Arimathea and Nicodemus laid his body on this slab of stone, anointed it with fragrant oils, and wrapped it in shrouds. The sheet on which Jesus was laid after being taken down off the cross, still bearing the imprint of his body and drops of his blood, is kept today at the Convent of the Sisters of Zion in Jerusalem.

Pilgrims belonging to the Eastern churches used to bring here shrouds that they spread over the stone and then saved for their own burials. Present-day pilgrims pour scented oil on the stone, soak it up in a cloth, and then wring the oil out into small bottles. Some come with a bag of tiny crucifixes, which they dip into the oil they pour on the stone.

148-154 ◇ The Holy Tomb
Jesus was buried close to the site of the crucifixion in a tomb cut in a rock belonging to Joseph of Arimathea. When the Church of the Holy Sepulcher was erected, the tomb was separated from the rock surrounding it and a magnificent rotunda was built around it. During the Crusader period, the edifice was renovated and the tomb overlaid with marble. In 1808, the dome of the rotunda collapsed in a fire that caused damage to the tomb as well.

The structure that presently surrounds the tomb was built by the Greek Orthodox after the nineteenth-century fire. It is divided into two parts: an anteroom known as the Chapel of the Angel, and the Chapel of the Holy Tomb. The empty tomb, covered by a cracked marble slab, is located on the right of the inner chamber. The chamber is small, and only three to four people can enter it at one time, which is why there is always a long line of believers at the entrance of the tomb.

155 ◇ The Garden Tomb in Jerusalem
The Anglicans identify a burial cave with two chambers on this spot as the burial place of Jesus. The cave, which was discovered by the German archaeologist Conrad Schick, is carved in a rock whose shape suggests that of a skull. In 1882, the British general Charles Gordon identified the rock as Golgotha (from *gulgolet*, the Hebrew word for skull). Today the site is maintained by the Anglican Church.

156 ◇ On the Threshold of the Holy Tomb
See 148-154.

157 ◇ The Catholic Ceremony of the Holy Fire in the Church of the Holy Sepulcher
This ceremony, which takes place on the first Saturday of Easter (according to the Gregorian calendar), commemorates the miracle of Jesus' disappearance from his tomb after his burial: "After the Sabbath, at dawn on the first day of the week, Mary Magdalene and the other Mary went to look at the tomb. There was a violent earthquake, for an angel of the Lord came down from heaven . . . His appearance was like lightning . . ." (Matthew 28:1-3).

The Patriarch stands in prayer before a censer of burning coals, onto which incense is poured in order to ignite the Holy Fire.

158-161 ◇ The Greek Orthodox Ceremony of the Holy Fire in the Church of the Holy Sepulcher

For the Eastern churches, the Ceremony of the Holy Fire is the most important of the Easter rites. It takes place on the first Saturday of Easter (according to the Julian calendar).The Greek Orthodox ceremony is the most striking. At its culmination, the Patriarch withdraws inside the Holy Tomb, carrying an unlit torch. While he prays, it is claimed, a flame descends from heaven and ignites the torch.

Outside the tomb, two representatives of the Armenian and Greek Orthodox Churches await the Patriarch's return, each of them holding an unlit torch. Thousands of believers throng the church and the adjoining plaza, carrying special tapers composed of thirty-three smaller candles–one for each year of Jesus' life on earth. The Patriarch passes the flame through two apertures in the wall of the Holy Tomb, enabling the Armenian and Greek Orthodox prelates to light their torches. These are then used to light the tapers of the faithful, who pass on the flame until everyone's candle is lit.

162-163 ◇ The Church of Emmaus in El-Qubeibeh

"Now that same day two of them were going to a village called Emmaus, about seven miles from Jerusalem. They were talking with each other about all that had happened. As they talked and discussed these things with each other, Jesus himself came up and walked along with them; but they were kept from recognizing him. He asked them, 'What are you discussing together as you walk along?' They stood still, their faces downcast. One of them, named Cleopas, asked him, 'Are you only a visitor to Jerusalem and do not know the things that have happened there in these days?' 'What things?' he asked. 'About Jesus of Nazareth,' they replied. 'He was a prophet, powerful in word and deed before God and all the people. The chief priests and our rulers handed him over to be sentenced to death, and they crucified him; but we had hoped that he was the one who was going to redeem Israel. And what is more, it is the third day since all this took place. In addition, some of our women amazed us. They went to the tomb early this morning but didn't find his body. They came and told us that they had seen a vision of angels, who said he was alive. Then some of our companions went to the tomb and found it just as the women had said, but him they did not see.' He said to them, 'How foolish you are, and how slow of heart to believe all that the prophets have said! Did not the Christ have to suffer these things and then enter his glory?' And beginning with Moses and all the prophets, he explained to them what was said in all the Scriptures concerning himself. As they approached the village to which they were going, Jesus acted as if he were going further. But they urged him strongly, 'Stay with us, for it is nearly evening; the day is almost over.' So he went in to stay with them" (Luke 24:13-29).

Over the years, several sites have been identified as ancient Emmaus, but today the most accepted is the village of El-Qubeibeh, about eleven kilometers northwest of Jerusalem. In the twelfth century, a church, a monastery, and a fortress were built in El-Qubeibeh. Excavations have shown that there was a settlement on the site during the time of Jesus.

The current church was built at the beginning of the twentieth century over the remains of the Crusader church in an effort to preserve its contours. The church is divided into a nave and two aisles–into the one on the left, the remains of a building identified as the home of Cleopas, who hosted Jesus, were incorporated. In the eastern portion, the apses from the Crusader period have been preserved. In the apse of the nave is a central altar shaped like a sarcophagus.

164-165 ◇ Emmaus in the Ajalon Valley

The village of Emmaus on the eastern edge of the Ajalon Valley has preserved its name since the Roman period. Early Christians identified it with the Emmaus mentioned in Luke, and a splendid Byzantine church, as well as a Crusader church, were built on the site, though they were later destroyed. There are many who still consider the identification valid and continue to make pilgrimages to Emmaus. On Easter Monday a mass is performed among the ruins of the Crusader church.

166-168 ◇ The Church of the Primacy of Peter in Tabgha

"Early in the morning, Jesus stood on the shore, but the disciples did not realize that it was Jesus. He called out to them, 'Friends, haven't you any fish?' 'No,' they answered. He said, 'Throw your net on the right side of the boat and you will find some.' When they did, they were unable to haul the net in because of the large number of fish. Then the disciple whom Jesus loved said to Peter, 'It is the Lord!' As soon as Simon Peter heard him say, 'It is the Lord,' he wrapped his outer garment around him (for he had taken it off) and jumped into the water. The other disciples followed in the boat, towing the net full of fish, for they were not far from shore, about a hundred yards. When they landed, they saw a fire of burning coals there with fish on it, and some bread. Jesus said to them, 'Bring some of the fish you just caught.' Simon Peter climbed aboard and dragged the net ashore. It was full of large fish, 153, but even with so many the net had not torn. Jesus said to them, 'Come and breakfast.' None of the disciples dared ask him, 'Who are you?' They knew it was the Lord. Jesus came, took the bread and gave it to them, and did the same with the fish" (John 21:4-13).

The Church of the Primacy of Peter is on the shore of the Sea of Galilee at Tabgha. According to tradition, this is where Jesus was revealed to his disciples after his death, where he dined with them, and where he gave the primacy to Peter.

The first church on this spot was built in the fourth century, and tradition attributes its construction to Helena, Emperor Constantine's mother. It was a small chapel with the holy stone called by pilgrims "Mensa Christi" (the Table of Christ) at its heart. It was destroyed at the end of the twelfth century, restored in the thirteenth century, and a short time afterwards, destroyed again. The present-day church was built by the Franciscans in 1939. To its south are the rock and the steps upon which, according to tradition, Jesus appeared after he was resurrected. Near the stairs, in the water, are double pillars that formerly adorned another edifice. They are known as "The Twelve Thrones" and are dedicated to the twelve disciples, who Jesus said would "sit on thrones, judging the twelve tribes of Israel" (Luke 22:30).

169 ◇ The Primacy of Peter

"When they had finished eating, Jesus said to Simon Peter, 'Simon son of John, do you truly love me more than these?' 'Yes, Lord,' he said. 'You know that I love you.' Jesus said, 'Feed my lambs.' Again Jesus said, 'Simon son of John, do you truly love me?' He answered, 'Yes, Lord, you know that I love you.' Jesus said, 'Tend my sheep.' The third time he said to him, 'Simon son of John, do you love me?' Peter was hurt because Jesus asked him a third time, 'Do you love me?' He said, 'Lord, you know all things; you know that I love you.' Jesus said, 'Feed my sheep. I tell you truly, when you were younger you dressed yourself and went where you wanted; but when you are old you will stretch out your hands, and someone else will dress you and lead you where you do not want to go'" (John 21:15-18).

The statue near the Church of the Primacy of Peter at Tabgha.

170-173 ◇ The Chapel of the Ascension on the Mount of Olives

Among the outstanding buildings commemorating Jesus' ascension to heaven was the Church of the Ascension on the Mount of Olives. Pilgrims have described its wonders since the fifth century, and despite the alterations it has undergone over the years, the church's location has not changed. The first church, which stood from the fourth to the tenth centuries, was circular in shape. On the inside of its wall was a colonnade encircling a small tube through which one could peer and see the footprint of Jesus. In place of the first church, the Crusaders built a church whose structure survives until today. It was surrounded by an octagonal wall in the form of a city wall, with watchtowers, crenellations, and embrasures: it was one of a string of fortresses that defended the Jerusalem-Jericho road. At its heart was an aedicule, designed with arches, double columns, and a dome open to the sky, symbolizing Jesus' ascension to heaven. In the center of the building was the stone from which Jesus rose to heaven, with his left footprint on it. After the defeat of the Crusaders, the church fell into Muslim ownership and was turned into a mosque. The dome was enclosed and the spaces between the pillars blocked up by walls. Later, the stone with the footprint was moved to the mosque's courtyard, and a small chapel built over it.

Once a year, on the anniversary of the Ascension, pilgrimage ceremonies of various Christian sects, which erect communion tables in the courtyard of the mosque, are held here.

174 ◇ The Cenacle

"When the day of Pentecost came, they were all together in one place. Suddenly a sound like the blowing of a violent wind came from heaven and filled the whole house where they were sitting. They saw what appeared to be tongues of fire that separated and came to rest on each of them. All of them were filled with the Holy Spirit and began to speak in other tongues as the Spirit enabled them" (Acts 2:1-4).

According to tradition, after Jesus' crucifixion the disciples would gather together with his mother and other believers. This church, in which the first core of believers assembled, is thus also called the Mother of All Churches. Jesus appeared before his disciples here after rising from the dead. The Holy Spirit also came to them here at Pentecost, after which they could speak the languages of all peoples, thus spreading the "good news." (See also 95-96.)

175 ◇ Pentecost. The mass in the Church of the Dormition

A pilgrimage is made to the Cenacle at Pentecost, when people gather for prayer at the nearby Church of the Dormition.

176 ◇ The Fountain in the Cloister of the Church of the Loaves and Fishes at Tabgha

Tabgha Valley extends to the northwest of the Sea of Galilee. The name of the valley, a corruption of the Greek word meaning "seven springs," originated in the seven springs that flowed in the valley in ancient times. The seven fish in the fountain symbolize the seven springs.